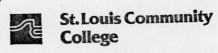

IDEAS IN ENGLISH

For Students of
English as a Second Language

ROBERT L. SAITZ
Boston University

FRANCINE B. STIEGLITZ
Boston University

WINTHROP PUBLISHERS, INC.
Cambridge, Massachusetts

Library of Congress Cataloging in Publication Data

Saitz, Robert L
    Ideas in English: for students of English as a
second language.

    1. English language—Text-books for foreigners.
2. Readers—1950-   I. Stieglitz, Francine B.,
1935-   joint author.   II. Title.
PE1128.S216   428'.2'4   74-6217
ISBN 0-87626-379-1

Copyright © 1974 by Winthrop Publishers, Inc.
    17 Dunster Street, Cambridge, Massachusetts
    02138

CONTENTS

v

PREFACE TO STUDENTS

This book is a collection of short readings in English which were written by twentieth-century authors. Most of the authors are contemporary, and all of them are considered good writers. They come from the United States, Great Britain, Canada, Australia, and India.

We chose these particular readings because we think that they are interesting and significant. The readings are about a variety of people, about how they think, how they feel, how they talk, and how they live.

The selections are not simplified. This means that some parts will be difficult. We have explained most of the idioms and difficult references, but we have not explained words that you can easily look up in a dictionary. Most of you will probably have to use a dictionary as you read these original selections, and we recommend an English-English dictionary such as *The Advanced Learner's Dictionary of Current English* by Hornby, Gatenby, and Wakefield or *The American Heritage Dictionary*.

We have also included language exercises that should encourage you to use English to say and write things about yourself, your ideas, your feelings, and your culture. We hope that you will enjoy both the readings and the exercises. We enjoyed preparing them.

RLS
FBS

PREFACE

This book is intended as a low intermediate level reader, with selections of high interest and low reading difficulty, for use in English language classes with secondary, college, or adult education students who have a limited command of English. The book focuses on the English language as a language in which significant ideas, attitudes, and observations can be communicated and makes such uses of the language available to students who have recently started to learn it.

We have chosen our selections from imaginative writing of the twentieth century. Our criteria for selection were (1) a high quality of writing, (2) a concern with subject matter that would engage the minds and feelings of contemporary readers, (3) a concern with themes that have a universal relevance, (4) a simplicity of vocabulary and sentence structure, (5) brevity, and (6) inclusion of a range of writers from varied cultural backgrounds. The language of the selections has not been revised or simplified; some of the selections are not the complete original works, but all retain the language of the author.

Accompanying each selection are (1) a brief lexical and cultural gloss, (2) comprehension questions, (3) suggestions for language exercises which emphasize the *use* of language, and (4) suggestions for writing. The gloss includes idiomatic expressions and cultural allusions that might be difficult for students to find in dictionaries. But since the selections have not been simplified and since words easy to find in dictionaries have not been glossed, it is anticipated that students will find it necessary to consult dictionaries. The comprehension section includes a range of questions, from the simple yes–no questions to the questions requiring analytical and imaginative responses. The teacher naturally will select those questions most appropriate to his or her students. In addition, the questions are arranged so that the teacher can use them as a controlled writing exercise; if students write out the answers to the questions in their present sequence, they will have a written summary of the main ideas or actions in the selection. The language exercises offer the teacher or learner a variety of oral and written activities which can be the basis for individual and group practice in discussions, games, and home assignments.

Although each selection is a self-contained unit and the book may be used in any order which proves interesting to the readers, the selections have been arranged in what we feel is the order of increasing difficulty.

CREDITS

THE OYSTER

Rumer Godden

Rumer Godden (b. 1907) is a British author who lives in England and in India. She has written many stories and novels about life in India, and she writes very well about nature and human nature. Among her popular works are Kingfishers Catch Fire *and* Two Under the Indian Sun *(an autobiography).*

The following selection is from one of her more recent books, Mooltiki: Stories and Poems from India. *In the story from which this selection comes, "The Oyster," Gopal is an Indian student studying in London. On a trip to France he goes to a restaurant with a friend who orders raw (live) oysters. Gopal feels that he has to eat the oysters although he does not like them. Suddenly the shock of all his new experiences begins to affect him. In the selection below, he is writing home and trying to describe his feelings.*

Up to this evening, which should have been the most delightful of all, everything had been delightful. "Delightful" was Gopal's new word. "London is delightful," he wrote home. "The college is delightful, Professor William Morgan is delightful and so is Mrs. Morgan and the little Morgans, but perhaps," he added with pain, for he had to admit that the Morgan children were rough and spoiled, "perhaps not *as* delightful if you see them for a very long time. . . . The hostel is

1

delightful. . . . I find my work delightful." He had planned to write home that Paris was delightful. "We went to a famous French restaurant in the rue Perpignan," he had meant to write, "it is called the Chez Perpignan. It is de—" Now tears made his dark eyes bright; he could not write that; it was not delightful at all.

GLOSS

up to: until
spoiled: badly behaved
hostel: a building for students where a room and meals are provided at low cost

A. COMPREHENSION

1. How long had everything been delightful?
2. Was Gopal a native of London? How do you know?
3. Why was Gopal in London?
4. Did Gopal like London?
5. Did Gopal like the Morgan children? Did he like them as much as he liked Professor Morgan and his wife?
6. Did Gopal write a letter home about London?
7. Did Gopal write a letter home about Paris?
8. What had Gopal planned to write about Paris?
9. Where did Gopal go "this evening"?
10. What do you think happened that made Gopal cry?

B. LANGUAGE EXERCISES

1. CONNECTING IDEAS

The following sentences are not in a normal order. Arrange them in an order that shows how the ideas are connected. You can combine sentences and add connectives if you think it will be better. You may be able to use such connectives as *then* or *after*.

Example: I fell asleep.
I drank some wine.
I had a delightful dream.

After I drank some wine, I fell asleep. Then I had a delightful dream.

a) He studied medicine there.
b) He had to return.
c) Before that he had lived in Paris.
d) He lived in New York for two years.
e) Now he could not stay away from home any longer.

2. FAVORITE WORDS

Often when we learn a new language we find a favorite word and we use it a lot. Gopal, for example, has discovered the word "delightful."

a) What are some English words that you use a lot?
b) What is an English word that you have learned and that you like the sound of?

3. "TO TRAVEL IS TO BROADEN THE MIND"

Living in a new place affects people differently. Some things which affect the experience of a person in a new place are the place itself, the age of the person, the purpose of the trip, and the length of time away from home.

a) How old do you think Gopal is?
b) How does travel affect young people? old people? children?
c) Gopal is unhappy. When people are away on a trip for a long time, what kinds of things make them unhappy?
d) Have you ever left your country to study or to travel? Was it a delightful experience?

(1) List some things that you found delightful and some that were not delightful.

Example: *Delightful*   *Not delightful*
eating new foods   losing my luggage

(2) Tell why you didn't like some of the things which you listed as not delightful in (1).

Example: Losing my luggage cost me a lot of money.

4. LETTERS HOME

a) Most people have trouble when they write letters home. What are some reasons for this difficulty?
b) Do you write different kinds of letters to different people? For example, what kinds of things do you write to your friends? To your parents? To other relatives?

5. SPOILED CHILDREN

Gopal thinks that the Morgan children are spoiled.

a) What do you think spoiled means for Gopal?
b) What does spoiled mean for you?
c) How do you think children should behave?

6. SENTENCE COMBINING

This is an exercise in combining three short sentences into one longer and better sentence. Your final sentence should have the same ideas as the original sentences, but you may make changes.

Example: (1) The children were delightful.
(2) The children were rough.
(3) The children were spoiled.

The children were delightful, but they were rough and spoiled.

a) (1) Professor Morgan is delightful.
   (2) Mrs. Morgan is delightful.
   (3) The children are not as delightful.

b) (1) He planned to write home.
   (2) He planned to write that everything was delightful.
   (3) He couldn't write that everything was delightful.

c) (1) He liked Paris.
   (2) He liked London better.
   (3) London was more like home.

C. SUGGESTIONS FOR WRITING

1. Imagine that you are visiting your favorite city away from home. Write a letter to your family describing your experiences in the city.
2. Imagine that you are visiting a city that you do not like. Write a letter to your family describing your unpleasant experiences.
3. What are some of the difficulties one encounters in a restaurant in an unfamiliar city? Describe an experience that you or a friend may have had.
4. Describe an experience which should have been better than it was.
5. Describe an experience which was better than you expected it to be.

HOW MY LOVE WAS SAWED IN HALF

Robert L. Fontaine

Robert L. Fontaine (1913–1965) was a Canadian-American who wrote plays, short stories and novels. His most famous work is The Happy Time, *which is about a French-Canadian family living in Ottawa in the 1920s. Fontaine's writing is usually humorous and he likes to use surprise endings as he does at the end of the first paragraph in the selection below.*

"How My Love Was Sawed in Half" appeared in The Atlantic Monthly *in 1960. It is the story of a young boy who runs away in the summertime to live with a carnival. The title of the story refers to one of Fontaine's experiences with the carnival: he fell in love with a girl who worked with a magician, and the magician used to pretend to saw the girl in half.*

When I was about twelve, or maybe I was fourteen, I ran away from home one summer. My home was a lovely, cool home. The bees would buzz in our flowerful back yard; great monarch butterflies would arch their way about the phlox and verbena. There would be watermelon on the vine,

6

and red tomatoes. It was all neatly arranged and predictable. That was why I ran away.

My mother and father, very strict parents indeed, thought I had gone to summer camp. My Uncle Louis, a great lover of good wine, thought I had gone to summer camp. All the neighbors thought so, too.

I started for summer camp, but I got off the train because I saw a carnival setting up. I intended to stay only until the next train north. Then I remembered the advice of my uncle: "If you do not see all of this world, you will not be ready for the next."

GLOSS

about: approximately

flowerful: the writer has invented this word to mean full of flowers

back yard: land in back of a house, usually enclosed by a fence or by trees and flowers

arch their way about the phlox and verbena: fly among the flowers

indeed: intensifies the meaning of *very strict*

summer camp: a place where groups of children play in the summer, with supervision

carnival: an amusement show that usually travels from place to place

setting up: preparing for a first performance

A. COMPREHENSION

1. What did Fontaine do one summer?
2. How old was he when he ran away from home?
3. Describe his home.
4. Did he live in a city?
5. Was there a garden in his back yard?
6. Were his parents strict?
7. Where did everyone think he had gone? Who were the people who thought so?
8. Did he start for camp?
9. How did he travel away from home?

10. Did he get off the train? Why?
11. Did he intend to stay at the carnival a long time?
12. Why did he run away?
13. What did the boy's uncle tell him?
14. What kind of person was Uncle Louis?
15. Do you think the boy went on the next train north?

B. LANGUAGE EXERCISES

1. VOCABULARY

a) Fill in the blanks using words from the list below. Some of
   the words may be used more than once.

advice	lovely	predictable
home	strict	about
neighbors	arranged	

The man at the carnival was very _____. He

wouldn't let me work there, but he gave me some

_____. He said, "Go _____." I arrived

home at _____ eight o'clock. Everything was still

_____ neatly and it looked _____.

b) Give another word or phrase, similar in meaning, that
   could replace the underlined words in the sentences below.

   (1) My home was a <u>very nice</u>, cool home.
   (2) It was all <u>carefully</u> arranged.
   (3) That was why I <u>left home.</u>
   (4) He was <u>approximately</u> ten years old.
   (5) <u>Perhaps</u> I was tired.
   (6) Everyone thought <u>in a similar way.</u>
   (7) John was going to be there, <u>also.</u>
   (8) They will <u>remain</u> here two more months.
   (9) Be <u>prepared</u> for anything.
   (10) My <u>mother and father</u> were very strict.

2. CONNECTING IDEAS

The following sentences are not in a normal order. Arrange them in an order which shows how the ideas are connected. You can combine sentences if you think it will be better.

a) I wanted to stay for a little while.
b) I got off the train.
c) I started for summer camp.
d) I saw a carnival setting up.
e) I went home.
f) I decided not to stay.

3. TRUE OR FALSE

Tell whether the following statements are True (T) or False (F) or Not Mentioned (N) in the selection you have just read. If a statement is not true, change it so that it is true according to the selection.

a) Fontaine ran away from home in the spring.
b) Fontaine lived in a large city.
c) There was no earth around Fontaine's home.
d) Fontaine ran away from home because it was not neat.
e) Fontaine stayed in the summer camp for a while.
f) The summer camp was for both boys and girls.
g) Uncle Louis didn't like wine.

4. PREDICTABLE AND UNPREDICTABLE

Make a list of actions or situations which you would describe as predictable or unpredictable.

Example: *Predictable*   *Unpredictable*
My mother gives me   I never know when my
tea when I am sick.   brother will telephone me.

5. I THOUGHT SO, TOO

Make up statements that other students can respond to by saying, "I thought so, too," or, "*I* didn't think so."

Examples: I thought the boy lived in a nice house.
I thought so, too.

I thought the boy was about twenty years old.
I didn't think so.

6. HOMES

a) In the first paragraph, the author gives some details of the back yard of his home. List some details that remind you of some part of your home (a garden, a porch, a patio).
b) Choose a month or a season and tell about the weather, the flowers, the fruit, etc., that would be there in your city or town.
c) What do you think makes a home lovely?

7. SAYINGS

Are there sayings in your culture which have a meaning similar to the idea of Uncle Louis's in paragraph 3? Are there other sayings which illustrate an attitude toward life that is common for people in your culture?

8. SENTENCE COMBINING

This is an exercise in combining three short sentences into one longer and better sentence. Your final sentence should have the same ideas as the original sentences, but you may make changes.

Example: (1) The children were delightful.
(2) The children were rough.
(3) The children were spoiled.

The children were delightful, but they were rough and spoiled.

a) (1) My house was very neatly arranged.
   (2) My house was very predictable.
   (3) I ran away.
b) (1) I was fourteen.
   (2) I ran away from home.
   (3) I wanted to see the world.
c) (1) There were bees in the yard.
   (2) There were butterflies in the yard.
   (3) The yard was in back of the house.
d) (1) I started for summer camp.
   (2) I got off the train.
   (3) I saw a carnival setting up.
e) (1) My uncle was a lover of good wine.
   (2) My uncle thought I had gone to summer camp.
   (3) My parents thought I had gone to summer camp.

C. SUGGESTIONS FOR WRITING

1. Describe an experience of running away from home. You can describe your own experience or the experience of a friend or an experience you have read about.
2. Young people, and sometimes older people, too, run away from their homes. What are some reasons for people doing this?
3. Fontaine writes that his parents were strict. What kinds of attitudes do you think strict parents would have?
4. What should be the ideal relationship between parents and children?
5. How would you write this selection if the events happened in the wintertime?
6. How would you write this selection if the events happened in your country? In your composition you might answer questions such as:

   Where would the boy be going for the summer?
   Where would he run away to?
   How would he travel?

MAMA
AND THE
HOSPITAL

Kathryn Forbes

---

*Kathryn Forbes (1909–1966) was the pseudonym for
Kathryn McLean, an American writer. She wrote
many articles and scripts for radio.*

   *This selection is taken from her most well-known
book,* Mama's Bank Account. *The book, which is
semiautobiographical, describes the life of recent
immigrants from Norway to the United States and the
problems they have in adjusting to life in a new
country. In this selection, Mama's daughter Dagmar
is in the hospital but no one can visit her for the first
twenty-four hours because of the hospital rules. Mama
tries several times to visit her daughter but the nurse
will not let her in. Finally, as described below, Mama
finds a way to get in. She takes her daughter Katrin
with her. Katrin is telling the story.*

   We walked in so quietly that the nurse at the
desk didn't even look up. Mama motioned for me to
sit in the big chair by the door. While I watched—
mouth open in surprise—Mama took off her hat
and coat and gave them to me to hold. Only then did
I notice that she'd kept her apron on. She tiptoed
over to the big closet by the elevator and took out
a damp mop. She pushed the mop past the desk and
as the nurse looked up, Mama nodded brightly.

"Very dirty floors," Mama said.

"Yes. I'm glad they've finally decided to clean them," the nurse answered. She looked at Mama curiously. "Aren't you working late?"

Mama just pushed more vigorously, each swipe of the mop taking her farther and farther down the hall. I watched until she was out of sight and the nurse had turned back to writing in the big book. Then I saw that I had held Mama's hat so tightly, one side was all out of shape.

After a long time, Mama came back. Her eyes were shining.

While the nurse stared with amazement, Mama placed the mop neatly back in the closet, put on her hat and coat, and took my hand. As we turned to go out the door, Mama bowed politely to the nurse and said, "Thank you."

Outside, Mama told me: "Dagmar is fine. No fever. I felt her forehead."

"You *saw* her, Mama?"

"Of course. She wakened while I was with her. I told her about clinic rules, she will not expect us until tomorrow."

"You won't try to see her again," I asked, "before then?"

"Why," Mama said, "that would be against the rules. Besides, I have seen for myself that all goes well with her. Papa will not worry, now."

I swallowed hard.

"Is a *fine* hospital," Mama said happily.

Then she clicked her tongue disapprovingly. "But such floors! A mop is never good. Floors should be scrubbed with a brush."

GLOSS

was out of sight: could not be seen
is a fine hospital: it's a fine hospital; Mama is a native speaker of
    Norwegian

A. COMPREHENSION

1. Where did Mama and Katrin go?
2. Why didn't the nurse look up?
3. Where did Katrin sit?
4. What clothes did Mama take off?
5. What did she keep on?
6. What did she take out of the closet?
7. What did she say to the nurse?
8. Why did the nurse look at Mama curiously?
9. What did Mama do when she came back?
10. What did she say to the nurse?
11. What did Mama say about Dagmar?
12. What did she tell Dagmar?
13. Is Mama going to visit Dagmar before tomorrow? Why not?
14. What did Mama say about the floors of the hospital?

B. LANGUAGE EXERCISES

1. VOCABULARY

Fill in the blanks using words from the list below. Some of the words may be used more than once.

sight	books	put on	notice
desk	took off	pushed	about
apron	looked up	noticing	against
rules	took out	expecting	

Mama ＿＿＿＿＿＿ her hat and stood near the

nurse's ＿＿＿＿＿＿. But the nurse didn't ＿＿＿＿＿＿

her. Mama coughed and the nurse finally ＿＿＿＿＿＿.

Mama ＿＿＿＿＿＿ a package from her bag and said,

"It's for Dagmar and she is ＿＿＿＿＿＿ it." The nurse

said, "Sorry, it's ＿＿＿＿＿＿ the rules." Mama said,

"But I am her Mama." The nurse smiled and said, "Rules

are _____." Mama didn't smile but she _____

her hat and left.

2. CONNECTING IDEAS

The following sentences are not in a normal order. Arrange them in an order that shows how the ideas are connected. You can combine sentences. There may be more than one possible order for the sentences.

a) She took out a mop.
b) She went past the nurse.
c) "But the floors are dirty."
d) She went to the closet.
e) Then she came back.
f) She was happy.
g) "It's a nice hospital," she said.

3. TRUE OR FALSE

Tell whether the following statements are True (T) or False (F) or Not Mentioned (N) in the story you have just read. If a statement is not true, change it so that it is true according to the story.

a) Katrin was surprised when Mama took off her hat and coat.
b) The closet was beside the nurse's desk.
c) The nurse knew Mama's daughter Dagmar.
d) The nurse was surprised when Mama started to clean the floor.
e) The nurse was busy typing names from a book.
f) Katrin changed the shape of Mama's hat.
g) Papa was waiting outside the hospital.
h) Mama was not very polite to the nurse.
i) Mama thought it was a good hospital.
j) Dagmar had been in the hospital for two weeks.

4. CURES

Dagmar had a fever. The doctor probably put something cool on her head to make her feel better.
What are some cures for the following problems?

Example:　　　　fever　　　　　　　　a cold towel on the head
- a) a sore throat
- b) a stuffed nose
- c) a backache
- d) a stomachache
- e) the hiccups
- f) diarrhea
- g) fingernail biting

5. RULES

- a) In the story, no visitors are allowed to see patients in the hospital for the first twenty-four hours. What other rules are there in hospitals?
- b) What are some rules that you will find in places such as schools, libraries, and parks?

6. TRICKS

Mama uses a trick to get into the hospital. She fools the nurse.

- a) Tell about a trick that you have used or that you know about.
- b) Tell about a trick that happened in something that you read. For example, one of the most famous tricks was the Trojan horse which the Greeks used to get into Troy.
- c) Another famous trick is the one that is told in Aesop's Fables about the fox and the crow.

　　A crow stole a piece of cheese and flew to a high tree to eat it. A fox sat under the tree and said to the crow: "You are a very beautiful bird. Your feathers are nice and white. And you probably have a beautiful voice." The crow was happy and very proud. Then the fox said, "Please sing for me." The crow decided to sing for the fox to show him her lovely voice. When she opened her mouth to sing, the cheese fell out. The fox ate the cheese and ran away laughing.

(1) If you have stories like this in your culture, tell one.

(2) This story is about a crow that was too proud. Do you have any stories or sayings in your culture about people who were too proud?

d) Many stories for children have tricks in them.

Once upon a time a king had a party and he invited everybody. He said that each person had to come *with and without* a present. Many people did not come because they could not do this. But one young girl came with something in her hands. "Put out your hand," she said to the king. The king put out his hand. Then the girl opened her hands and a little bird flew away.

(1) Did the girl come *with and without* a present?

(2) Tell a story that is usually told to children in your culture.

e) Here is a trick which is famous in many cultures.

A young man was walking along a road and he had a long way to walk. He saw a man coming on a horse so he took off his hat and put it on the road. Then he put his hands on the hat. When the man on the horse came along and saw this, he asked, "What do you have under that hat?" The young man answered, "A beautiful golden bird." The man said, "Let me see it." The young man said, "I don't want to lose it. Let me take your horse. If you will wait here and hold this hat down, I'll go and get a cage for the bird." The man got off his horse and held the hat down. The young man got on the horse and went away. The man waited and waited— and waited. Finally he looked under the hat. There was nothing.

7. SENTENCE COMBINING

This is an exercise in combining three short sentences into one longer and better sentence. Your final sentence should have the same ideas as the original sentences, but you may make changes.

Example:
    (1) The children were delightful.
    (2) The children were rough.
    (3) The children were spoiled.

The children were delightful, but they were rough and spoiled.

a) (1) I got to the desk.
    (2) The nurse looked up.
    (3) The nurse motioned for me to sit.

b) (1) She went over to the closet.
    (2) She took out a damp mop.
    (3) She started to clean the floor.

c) (1) Mama took off her hat.
    (2) Mama took off her coat.
    (3) Mama gave me her hat and coat to hold.

d) (1) The nurse stared at Mama.
    (2) Mama placed the mop in the closet.
    (3) Mama put on her hat and coat.

e) (1) We started to go out the door.
    (2) Mama bowed politely to the nurse.
    (3) Mama said, "Thank you."

f) (1) I was with my cousin.
    (2) My cousin awakened.
    (3) I told my cousin about the clinic rules.

C. SUGGESTIONS FOR WRITING

1. Describe an experience that you or a friend has had in a hospital.
2. Retell the story in 6(e) as if the man were telling what happened to him.

Example: I was riding on my horse one day. . . .

3. Retell a fable, a trick, or a children's story from your culture.
4. Retell the story of the visit to the hospital from Mama's point of view.

   Example: I was worried about Dagmar and I wanted to see her.

IN A STRANGE TOWN

Sherwood Anderson

Sherwood Anderson (1876–1941) was an American novelist and short story writer. Much of his writing describes life in the small towns of the United States. Probably his most popular work is Winesburg, Ohio, *a collection of stories about people who lived in the midwestern section of the United States earlier in this century.*

The following passage is from "In a Strange Town," which first appeared in the January 1930 issue of Scribner's *magazine. In "In a Strange Town," Anderson tells of his feelings as he travels to different places in the United States and observes parts of the lives of other people. In the following passage, he remembers a fragment of life in his home town.*

The style of this passage is conversational as the author pretends to talk to himself.

There is a particular house in that street—in my home town—I was formerly very curious about. For some reason the people who lived in it were recluses. They seldom came out of their house and hardly ever out of the yard, into the street.

Well, what of all that?

My curiosity was aroused. That is all.

I used to walk past the house with something

strangely alive in me. I had figured out this much. An old man with a beard and a white-faced woman lived there. There was a tall hedge and once I looked through. I saw the man walking nervously up and down, on a bit of lawn, under a tree. He was clasping and unclasping his hands and muttering words. The doors and shutters of the mysterious house were all closed. As I looked, the old woman with the white face opened the door a little and looked out at the man. Then the door closed again. She said nothing to him. Did she look at him with love or with fear in her eyes? How do I know? I could not see.

Another time I heard a young woman's voice, although I never saw a young woman about the place. It was evening and the woman was singing— a rather sweet young woman's voice it was.

There you are. That is all. Life is more like that than people suppose. Little odd fragmentary ends of things. That is about all we get. I used to walk past that place all alive, curious. I enjoyed it. My heart thumped a little.

I heard sounds more distinctly, felt more.

GLOSS

home town: place where a person was born and grew up
yard: land in front or back of a house usually enclosed by a fence or by trees and flowers
figured out: thought about until understood
about the place: near the house

A. COMPREHENSION

1. What was the narrator curious about?
2. Why was the narrator curious about the people?
3. Where did the narrator used to walk?

4. Who lived in the house?
5. What did the narrator look through?
6. What was the old man doing?
7. Were the doors and shutters opened or closed?
8. What did the old woman do?
9. Did the old woman say anything to the man?
10. Did she look at the man with love or fear?
11. Did the narrator ever see a young woman about the place?
12. What did the narrator hear one evening?
13. What did the narrator say about life?
14. How did the narrator feel when he walked past the place?

B. LANGUAGE EXERCISES

1. VOCABULARY

Fill in the blanks using words from the list below. Some of the words may be used more than once.

sounds	yard	distinctly	hear
shutters	lawn	formerly	figure out
recluses	particular	strangely	thumps
curiosity	odd	used to	matters
hedge	alive	enjoyed	suppose

I _____ ask my friends who the _____ were. My friends did not know, and gradually my _____ _____ died. I stopped looking through the _____ into the _____. I stopped walking down that _____ street. I stopped trying to _____ whether the two people loved or feared each other.

I will never forget that _____ bit of life. My heart still _____ when I hear a young woman singing. But I don't hear sounds so _____ now.

2. CONNECTING IDEAS

The following sentences are not in a normal order. Arrange them in an order that shows how the ideas are connected. You can combine sentences and add connectives if you think it will be better.

a) They were recluses.
b) An old man and woman lived in that house.
c) I used to walk past a particular house.
d) I never saw them on the street.
e) I saw them on the lawn.
f) Once I looked through a hedge.

3. VARYING THE THEME

Imagine that the story was different. What might have happened?

SITUATION	RESPONSE
The people in the house were not recluses.	They invited the author into the house.
The hedge was short.	
The man was young.	
The young woman was crying.	
The author was not curious.	

4. CURIOSITY

a) Are there things that make you, or have made you, curious about your neighbors?

Example: The lights in the house next to mine are on all night.

b) Are you curious about what your neighbors do?

Example: I am curious about where my neighbor works.

c) Have you ever figured out something about somebody?

Example: I figured out that he lives alone.

d) List things that you are curious about.

Example: I would like to know how a television works.

5. HOME TOWN LIFE

a) What little things do you remember about the houses in your home town?

Example: I remember a house with purple shutters.

b) Name a place and ask your friend or classmate, "What is the first thing that you think of?"

Example: Paris   fresh bread in the morning

6. SENTENCE COMBINING

This is an exercise in combining three short sentences into one longer and better sentence. Your final sentence should have the same ideas as the original sentences, but you may make changes.

Example: (1) The children were delightful.
     (2) The children were rough.
     (3) The children were spoiled.

     The children were delightful, but they were rough and spoiled.

a) (1) I saw a man.
 (2) The man was walking nervously.
 (3) The man was walking on the lawn.
b) (1) He was clasping his hands.
 (2) He was unclasping his hands.
 (3) He was muttering words.

c) (1) I was looking at the house.
   (2) The woman opened the door.
   (3) The woman looked out at the man.
d) (1) I heard a voice.
   (2) It was a young woman's voice.
   (3) I never saw a young woman there.
e) (1) An old man lived there.
   (2) The old man had a beard.
   (3) The beard was grey.
f) (1) I used to walk past that house.
   (2) I was curious.
   (3) I was alive.

C. SUGGESTIONS FOR WRITING

1. Describe the life on your particular street.
2. Write a description of a mysterious couple or a mysterious person.
3. Describe an incident that made you very curious.

NOT
GOIN'
ANYWHERE

Darryl Ponicsan

---

*Darryl Ponicsan (b. 1938) is a young American author
who lives in California. He has a Master of Arts degree
from Cornell University and has taught in American
schools. He has written several novels.*

The following selection is taken from Andoshen,
Pa. *(Pa. is an abbreviation for Pennsylvania), a novel
which describes life in a small town in the state of
Pennsylvania. The title of the selection, which is the
title of one of the chapters in the novel, reflects the
feelings of some of the people in the town who think
that their lives are not happy because everything
always seems the same. In this selection we read about
Estelle Wowak, a young girl who dreams of the time
when she will leave her useless job in a small town and
go to live and work in New York.*

Estelle ran the scene over and over again in
her imagination because some day soon she was
actually going to break in a new girl. She was going
to go to New York. She was going to get a room
right in the city and find a job as a secretary, and if
she couldn't find one, she would go to the five and
dime, there must be fifty of them in New York, and
with her experience she would have no trouble
getting a job. Working in the five and dime in New

York is not like working in the five and dime in Andoshen. There you're really dealing with the public. You probably never see the same customer twice.

She would get a room in the middle of the city, and every night she would walk down Broadway and once a week she would go to Radio City Music Hall, on Saturday, and to the zoo on Sunday. After a while she would be like any other city person, and strangers would stop her on the street and ask for directions to the Statue of Liberty. She would tell them (because she would know) in a clipped, familiar way, and measure the distance in minutes instead of miles, like a city person.

GLOSS

ran the scene over and over again: practiced or rehearsed the scene many times

break in (a person): train; teach a job (to someone)

five and dime: a store that sells a variety of inexpensive things; at one time, such stores sold things for five and ten cents

dealing with: meeting

a clipped, familiar way: Estelle thinks that people in New York shorten their words and talk very informally

A. COMPREHENSION

1. Did Estelle daydream about leaving her job?
2. How was Estelle's replacement going to learn her job?
3. Where was Estelle going to go?
4. Was she going to get an apartment in the suburbs?
5. What kind of job was she going to look for?
6. If she couldn't find a job as a secretary, what would she do?
7. Would she have trouble getting a job? Why?
8. Did Estelle see the same customers in Andoshen? Why?
9. Would she see the same people in New York?
10. What would Estelle do at night in New York?
11. What would she do on Saturday?

12. What would she do on Sunday?
13. Why would strangers stop her on the street?
14. What does Estelle mean when she says that she would "measure the distance in minutes instead of miles"?
15. How do city people measure distance?

B. LANGUAGE EXERCISES

1. VOCABULARY

Give another word or phrase similar in meaning that could replace the underlined words in the sentences below.

a) She rehearsed the scene in her mind.
b) The manager trained the new employee.
c) We inquired how to go to the Statue of Liberty.
d) He had no difficulty finding work.
e) A salesperson does business with persons who buy things.
f) After some time, she got a job.

2. CONNECTING IDEAS

The following sentences are not in a normal order. Arrange them in an order that shows how the ideas are connected. You can connect sentences if you think it will be better.

a) He had trouble understanding city people.
b) After a while, he went home again.
c) He didn't like working in the five and dime.
d) He went to New York.
e) He decided to quit his job.
f) He couldn't find a job.

3. VARYING THE THEME

Imagine that the story was different. What might have happened?

SITUATION	RESPONSE
Estelle's cousin went to New York with her.	

Estelle didn't like New York.

Estelle didn't quit her job.

Estelle ran away to the capital of your country.

4. THINGS I'VE ALWAYS WANTED TO DO

People always dream of things they want to do.

a) Make a list of three things that you have always wanted to do. For each thing, tell why you haven't done it yet.
b) Get suggestions from the rest of the class or from friends on how to do these things.

5. THE CITY AND THE TOWN

a) People who live in big cities often dream of living in small towns or in the country. People who live in small towns or in the country often dream of living in big cities. List the good and bad points of living in cities and in small towns.
b) If you ran away to another city, where would you go and what would you do?
c) What can you do so that you won't become lonely in a big city? In a small town?
d) The writer feels that city people measure distance in minutes, not in miles. What are some other specific differences between life in a big city and life in a small town?
e) Compare big cities in the world.
f) What kinds of jobs are available in a big city? In a small town? In the country?

6. SENTENCE COMBINING

This is an exercise in combining three short sentences into one longer and better sentence. Your final sentence should have the same ideas as the original sentences, but you may make changes.

Example: (1) The children were delightful.
              (2) The children were rough.
              (3) The children were spoiled.

The children were delightful, but they were rough and spoiled.

a) (1) She was going to go to New York.
    (2) She was going to get a room right in the city.
    (3) She was going to find a job as a secretary.

b) (1) She worked in the five and dime.
    (2) She found another job.
    (3) She found a job as a secretary.

c) (1) New York is better than Andoshen.
    (2) New York is big.
    (3) Andoshen is small.

d) (1) She would go to Broadway on Wednesday.
    (2) She would go to the zoo on Saturday.
    (3) She would go to concerts on Sunday.

e) (1) Strangers thought she was a city person.
    (2) Strangers stopped her on the street.
    (3) Strangers asked her for directions.

C. SUGGESTIONS FOR WRITING

1. Compare Estelle to the boy who ran away from home one summer (in the selection "How My Love Was Sawed in Half"). Who was more adventurous?
2. Describe the first job you had. Was it boring? Was it difficult?
3. Imagine that you worked in a five and dime store. Describe your job.
4. Sometimes people are disappointed when they finally do the things that they have always wanted to do. Describe one experience like that; it can be your experience or the experience of a friend.

LEAF

William Saroyan

William Saroyan (b. 1908) is an American writer of Armenian background who has written short stories, plays and novels. He writes mostly about the very different ways in which people enjoy daily life in the United States. The Daring Young Man on the Flying Trapeze, *a collection of stories, is probably one of his best-known works.*

This selection is taken from the book Papa, You're Crazy. *In that book Saroyan describes a boy and his father who go to different places in San Francisco and enjoy the experiences of everyday life.*

At last we went out and stood on the lawn and watched the sun go down, and my father said, "If it weren't for art, we'd have vanished from the face of the earth long ago."

What art *really* is, though, and what a human being really is, and what the world really is, I just don't *know,* that's all.

Standing there, watching the sun go down into the sea, my father said, "In every house there ought to be an art table on which, one by one, things are placed, so that everybody in that house might look at the things very carefully, and *see* them."

"What would *you* put on a table like that?"

"A leaf. A coin. A button. A stone. A small piece of torn newspaper. An apple. An egg. A pebble. A flower. A dead insect. A shoe."

"Everybody's *seen* those things."

"Of course. But nobody *looks* at them, and that's what art is. To look at familiar things as if they had never before been seen. A plain sheet of paper with typing on it. A necktie. A pocketknife. A key. A fork. A cup. A bottle. A bowl. A walnut."

"What about a baseball? A baseball's a beautiful thing."

"It certainly is. You would place something on the table and look at it. The next morning you would take it away, and put something else there— *anything,* for there is nothing made by nature or by man that doesn't deserve to be looked at particularly."

Now, the sun was gone all the way into the sea. There was a lot of orange light on the water, and in the sky above the water. Legion of Honor Hill grew dark, and my father brought out a cigarette and lighted it and inhaled and then let the smoke out of his nose and mouth, and he said, "Well, boy, there's another day of the wonderful world gone forever."

"*New* day tomorrow, though."

"What do you say we drive to the Embarcadero and look at the ships from all over the world?"

GLOSS

at last: finally

What do you say we drive: let's drive

A. COMPREHENSION

1. Where were the narrator and his father standing as the selection begins?
2. What did they watch?
3. Does the narrator know what art really is?
4. The father says that there should be something in every house. What?

5. Why should there be things on the table?
6. What are some things the father would put on the table?
7. What is something the narrator would put on the table?
8. How long would the father leave something on the table?
9. Does the father believe that there are some things which do not deserve to be looked at?
10. Why was there a lot of orange light on the water?
11. What did the father suggest that they do the next day?
12. What is the father's attitude toward life?

B. LANGUAGE EXERCISES

1. VOCABULARY

Fill in the blanks using words from the list below. Some of the words may be used more than once.

watch	preserve	wonderful
look	familiar	art
see	beautiful	earth

A tree is certainly a _____ object, but not

many people would call it an object of _____.

While people pay to _____ a sports event, very

few would pay to _____ at a tree. But if you look

at a _____ tree in the springtime, you will _____

_____ many things you haven't seen before. You may

decide that a tree is a _____ thing.

2. CONNECTING IDEAS

The following sentences are not in a normal order. Arrange them in an order that shows how the ideas are connected. You can combine sentences and add connectives if you think it will be better.

- a) We watched the sun.
- b) Another day was gone.
- c) The sun went down.
- d) We stood on the lawn.
- e) The sky was full of orange light.
- f) We went outside.
- g) The place grew dark.

3. LOOK AND SEE

During a day we see many things but often we do not look at them carefully. Look carefully at something that you see every day and describe it.

Example: I am standing in an elevator. Everybody is looking at the floor or at the ceiling. Nobody is looking at anybody.

4. FAMILIAR THINGS

- a) What are some familiar things that you do not see now? They may be things that were in your home or your country or things that existed during your childhood.
- b) What are some unfamiliar things or customs that you have seen recently?
- c) Choose a familiar object and bring it to class, but do not show it to the class. Describe it to the class and see if they can guess what it is from your description.

5. ART

The father of the narrator believes that art is a way of giving special attention to the familiar things of life.

- a) What are some paintings that illustrate this idea of art?

b) What are some stories or novels or poems in your culture that illustrate this idea of art?

c) Do you agree with the father's idea?

d) Do you know any paintings or writings that illustrate a different idea of art?

e) The father says that there ought to be an art table in every home. What would you put on such a table?

6. FATHERS AND SONS

The narrator and his father seem to spend a lot of time together.

a) What kinds of things do fathers and sons do together in your culture?

b) Riddle: A little boy is the son of a doctor but the doctor is not the father of the little boy. What is the relationship between the boy and the doctor?

(If you can't guess, the answer is on page 129.)

7. SENTENCE COMBINING

This is an exercise in combining three short sentences into one longer and better sentence. Your final sentence should have the same ideas as the original sentences, but you may make changes.

Example: (1) The children were delightful.
(2) The children were rough.
(3) The children were spoiled.

The children were delightful, but they were rough and spoiled.

a) (1) My father lighted a cigarette.
(2) We stood on the lawn.
(3) We watched the sun go down.

b) (1) I don't know what art is.
(2) I don't know what a human being is.
(3) I don't know what the world is.

c) (1) My father was standing there.
   (2) My father was watching the sun go down.
   (3) My father said, "Every house should have an art table."

d) (1) Every house should have an art table.
   (2) Everybody could look at things carefully.
   (3) Everybody could really see things.

e) (1) My father said something.
   (2) "Everybody's seen familiar things."
   (3) "Nobody looks at them."

f) (1) Everybody has seen a flower.
   (2) Everybody has seen a stone.
   (3) Nobody looks at those things.

g) (1) My father took out a cigarette.
   (2) My father inhaled the smoke.
   (3) My father let the smoke out of his nose and mouth.

C. SUGGESTIONS FOR WRITING

1. Describe a day or part of a day when you and your father had a good time together.
2. The father thinks that the world is wonderful. Describe someone you know who has a similar attitude.
3. Describe someone you know who has an attitude toward life which is very different from the father's.
4. What do you think the father meant when he said, "If it weren't for art, we'd have vanished from the face of the earth long ago"?

JONES
BEACH

Nicholas Gagarin

Nicholas Gagarin (b. 1948) grew up in Connecticut and attended Harvard College, where he wrote for the campus newspaper.

The following selection was taken from Gagarin's novel Windsong, *a story of young people and the ways they experience life. "Jones Beach," which is the title of a chapter in the novel, is a public beach on Long Island, New York. In the reading below, the author describes the wonderful feeling of freedom he has when he starts to drive to the beach one morning in June.*

Connecticut is beautiful in early June. The rolling hills are green and beckoning, the leaves on the trees full and deep. The land is fertile, washed and nourished by the spring rains; and in the rich soil of gardens, peas and carrots are appearing. The mornings are warm and clear, the sun rising early so that by midday you can get a taste of the summer heat that will follow in July and August.

On a day like this, on a Wednesday morning in early June, it is possible to feel free; for school is over for the year and the summer lies ahead. And so, on this Wednesday morning, you get up early in the morning and go out for a drive in your car, because you like that, it's fun. You drive along a little country road, the top of your car down, and you feel the chill of the early morning air, as the wind blows all around you. You feel the chill in your neck and behind your ears, but the sun is getting higher in the sky; it will be warmer soon. You feel your hair being blown in a thousand directions, and that's fine. It's good to feel the long brown hair blowing around your ears, it's good sometimes to look down onto the road next to your car and see the shadow of the car, with you inside, and your hair blowing in the wind. You drive through patches of sunlight and shade; the air is dry, so you feel the difference. And you feel free, being free.

It is hard to be free. It is probably one of the hardest things in the world, because the world doesn't leave much room for freedom. There isn't much space given you, there aren't many people around you who are free. Everyone has miles to go and things to do, and the world catches you up, it carries you along, it doesn't give you much room. But it's also so easy to be free. Being free is probably one of the easiest things in the world, too, only almost nobody realizes it. Because we are free: we were born free, we live free, and we will die free. Only we don't realize it. There is always so much going on, perhaps, always so much to do, that we never stop and look at what's happening. Until some day, some Wednesday morning in early June, when you get up in the morning when it's still chilly and you go for a drive in your car, along a country road, through little towns, past little homes and farmhouses, and suddenly you realize it, you know it: you are free, free always, free forever.

GLOSS
for: because
school is over: the school year is finished

the top of your car down: this refers to a car whose top can be
  folded—a convertible
the world catches you up: you become involved in many activities
going on: happening

A. COMPREHENSION

1. When does the story take place?
2. Why does the narrator feel free?
3. What does the narrator do one morning?
4. Where does he go?
5. Does the narrator feel warm or cold? Why?
6. Does the narrator have short hair or long hair?
7. What does the narrator like to do while he is driving?
8. Does the narrator think it is easy or hard to be free? Why?

B. LANGUAGE EXERCISES

1. VOCABULARY

Fill in the blanks with the words or phrases listed below. Some
of the words may be used more than once.

fun	free	realize
freedom	possible	blows
chill	easy	ahead
sunlight	drive	
air	feel	

Many people like to _____. They feel _____

_____ as they look _____ on the road and see

the _____. They _____ free as the

_____ _____ on their faces. They know

that it is _____ to drive, but many do not _____

_____ that their pleasure comes from a feeling of

_____.

2. CONNECTING IDEAS

The following sentences are not in a normal order. Arrange them in an order that shows how the ideas are connected. You may connect the sentences if you want to.

  a) School is over in June.
  b) It feels cool in the early morning air.
  c) You can drive every day.
  d) Then summer vacation begins.
  e) The air gets warmer when the sun gets higher.
  f) You can drive along a country road.
  g) The best feeling is that you are free.

3. WHAT DO YOU FEEL?

  a) Describe what you feel when you do the following things.

Example: _Situation:_ You ride in an open car.
          Response: You feel a chill on your back.

  Situations

  1) You step in a puddle.
  2) You fall into cold water.
  3) You lie in the sun for six hours.
  4) You go for a walk early in the morning.
  5) You walk in the street alone late at night.
  6) You ride with someone who drives very fast.
  7) You take a plane trip.

  b) Describe what you feel when the following things happen.
  1) School is over for the year.
  2) You win the lottery.
  3) Your parents are angry at you.

4) You don't eat breakfast.

5) You lose your money or your identification cards.

4. VACATIONS

   a) What do you like to do when you have a vacation?
      1) Where do you like to go?
      2) What do you like to wear?
      3) Do you like to be alone or with others?
      4) What do you like to eat?
   b) What kinds of vacations have you had?

5. POETRY

The following is an excerpt from the poem "Stopping by Woods on a Snowy Evening" by Robert Frost:

> The woods are lovely, dark and deep,
> But I have promises to keep,
> And miles to go before I sleep,
> And miles to go before I sleep.

   a) What do you think the author is talking about in this poem?
   b) Where has Gagarin expressed ideas similar to those expressed by Robert Frost?

6. SENTENCE COMBINING

This is an exercise in combining three short sentences into one longer and better sentence. Your final sentence should have the same ideas as the original sentences, but you may make changes.

Example: (1) The children were delightful.
           (2) The children were rough.
           (3) The children were spoiled.

The children were delightful, but they were rough and spoiled.

a) (1) I feel free.
   (2) School is over.
   (3) Summer lies ahead.

b) (1) I got up in the morning.
   (2) It was still chilly.
   (3) I went for a long walk.

c) (1) It was on a Wednesday morning.
   (2) It was early in June.
   (3) I realized I was free.

d) (1) We put the top of the car down.
   (2) We could feel the wind.
   (3) The wind was blowing all around us.

e) (1) You drive along a country road.
   (2) You have the top of your car down.
   (3) You feel the chill of the early morning air.

f) (1) The sun is in the sky.
   (2) The sun is moving higher.
   (3) It will be warmer soon.

g) (1) I like to drive along a country road.
   (2) I like to drive through little towns.
   (3) I like to drive past farmhouses.

h) (1) It is easy to live free.
   (2) It is easy to die free.
   (3) We don't realize that it is easy to live and die free.

i) (1) There is too much going on.
   (2) There is too much to do.
   (3) We never stop and look at what's happening.

C. SUGGESTIONS FOR WRITING

1. Describe a vacation that was not as successful as you had planned.
2. Describe a vacation that was better than you had expected it to be.
3. Imagine that the narrator of "Jones Beach" is now about 50 years old and he is telling what happened many years ago.

LIKE THE LION'S TOOTH

Marjorie Kellogg

Marjorie Kellogg (b. 1922) is an American writer who
grew up in rural California and studied psychology
in college. She has written a number of plays for
television and for the theater. Her first book, Tell Me
That You Love Me, Junie Moon, was very popular;
many critics called it beautiful and touching. The
author is good at creating characters that the reader does
not forget easily. Her personal philosophy is that "art,
like love, will survive all the abuse man can give
it. . . ."

Like the Lion's Tooth, which is her second novel,
is about a group of children who are at a special
school for children with problems. In the following
selection, Ben, who is at the school, remembers when
his family was together. The title of the novel comes
from a line in a poem by W. B. Yeats: "Love is
like the lion's tooth."

In the old days, when they were all together,
before his father went to sea, and was sober and not
accusing his mother of anything, they sometimes

took a picnic out to Long Beach and sat in the shade under the boardwalk. They were all fair and sunburned easily, all except Ben, who turned chocolate brown, and it was rare that their mother would even let them take off their shirts.

His old man would prop himself against a piling and sleep away the afternoon, and Sara, his mother, would sit looking out to sea, letting the sand sift through her fingers. Sometimes she would let Ben cover her with sand with only her head sticking out, and then he would decorate her with shells and seaweed and any other bright-colored trash he could find on the beach.

"I look like a birthday cake," Sara would say, smiling at his nonsense.

At the beach he always felt free and light on his feet. He would run and belly-dive the waves and swim out beyond the buoy until the people on the beach looked like black dots. Going out, he would swim on his back as though the sight of the beach were his anchor line.

"I was watching you," Sara would say. He would swell with pride.

At the beach, Philip played in the shade, digging quietly among the pilings, finding things everyone else had overlooked.

"Why don't you go in the water?" his mother would say. "Go on, Philly. It will do you good." Philip would never even look up. His mind was considering a rusty bracelet with blue and red stones.

When it was dark, they would gather up things for the trip home. Ben hated this time. Just once he wanted to stay until everyone had gone, when the beach was deserted.

"Daddy, Daddy," Winnie would shriek, "I can't *see!*" The pilings under the boardwalk looked like giants in the dark.

"Open your eyes, then," he would grumble.

"They *are* open, they *are!*" And she would tug at his pants until he would pick her up and carry her out to the street on his shoulders. From a distance, they all looked very happy.

GLOSS

sober: not drunk
boardwalk: a wooden structure for walking along above a beach
old man: a slang term for father
prop (himself) against: lean against
a piling: a heavy piece of wood supporting a structure, here the boardwalk
sleep away the afternoon: sleep the whole afternoon
belly-dive the waves: dive with the waves as they break
do you good: be good for you
his mind was considering: he was thinking about

A. COMPREHENSION

1. What did Ben's family sometimes do in the summer?
2. Did they sit in the sun?
3. Why didn't their mother let them take off their shirts?
4. What would Ben's father do?
5. What would Ben's mother do?
6. What did Ben like to do to his mother?
7. How did Ben feel at the beach?
8. Did Ben like to swim?
9. How far out would he swim?
10. Did he swim on his side or on his back?
11. Did Philip like to swim?
12. What did Philip like to do?
13. Why did Ben hate to leave the beach?
14. Why did Winnie tug at her father's pants?
15. How did Winnie's father carry her?

B. LANGUAGE EXERCISES

1. VOCABULARY

Fill in the blanks using words from the list below. Some of the words may be used more than once.

shade	boardwalk	cover	decorated
shells	waves	prop against	digging
beach	sit	deserted	tugging
pilings	sift	sunburned	considering

There are two kinds of people who go to the _____: those who like to sit in the sun and those who like to sit in the _____. Some people never go into the water. They just _____ on the sand. Others _____ themselves or their friends with sand. Still others spend their time _____ for _____. During the summer months, the beach is rarely _____.

2. COMPLETING AND CONNECTING IDEAS

a) Complete the following sentences using information from the selection. You do not have to use the same words as in the selection.
   (1) His father would sleep on the sand, and his mother . . .
   (2) Ben wanted to stay until . . .
   (3) Sara said, "I look like a . . ."
   (4) They sometimes took food to the beach and . . .
   (5) Winnie's father would pick her up and . . .
   (6) Ben would decorate his mother with . . .

(7) Philip's mother said to him, "Why don't you . . . ?"
(8) When it was dark, . . .
(9) Philip played in the shade, digging . . .
(10) He would swim out . . .

b) Arrange the sentences in a) in the order in which the ideas occur in the selection.

3. TRUE OR FALSE

Tell whether the following statements are True (T) or False (F) or Not Mentioned (N) in the story you have just read. If a statement is not true, change it so that it is true according to the story.

a) Ben's father became a sailor.
b) Everyone in the family had dark skin.
c) The family used to walk from their home to the beach.
d) Ben's mother liked to be at the beach.
e) Ben and his family were the only people at the beach.
f) Ben couldn't swim very well.
g) Philip swam very well.
h) Ben's father joked with the children.
i) The mother and the father were friendly toward each other.

4. ON THE BEACH

a) List the kinds of things you would find at a beach.

Example: a blanket

b) What kinds of activities do you like to do at a beach?

Example: run

c) What kinds of people do you see at a beach?

Example: people who are always eating

5. REMEMBERING

Ben remembers a happy time in his childhood when he felt free. Tell of a time in your childhood when you felt: free, proud, happy, sad, frustrated.

6. COMPARISONS

We often use comparisons to make our speech or writing more effective. For example, Sara says, "I look like a birthday cake."

    a) In this selection, what did the pilings look like to Winnie? What did the people on the beach look like to Ben?

    b) Describe someone you know (it can be a famous person) using a comparison.

    c) What do you think the phrase "Love is like the lion's tooth" means?

7. THEY ALL LOOKED VERY HAPPY

When the author writes that they all looked very happy, she seems to be saying that maybe they really were not very happy. We know that the father "grumbled" and that he spent all afternoon sleeping. We know that at a later time the father was not sober and that he accused the mother of something. If we read more of this story, we would find out that Philip is not a normal child.

What are some situations in which people act differently from how they feel?

Example: Children often whistle when they are afraid.

8. SENTENCE COMBINING

This is an exercise in combining three short sentences into one longer and better sentence. Your final sentence should have the same ideas as the original sentences, but you may make changes.

Example: (1) The children were delightful.
(2) The children were rough.
(3) The children were spoiled.

The children were delightful, but they were rough and spoiled.

a) (1) They were all together in the old days.
(2) They went to the beach in the old days.
(3) This was before their father went to sea.

b) (1) The girls were fair.
(2) The girls sunburned easily.
(3) The boy was dark.

c) (1) He sat in the sun.
(2) He got sunburned.
(3) His mother made him put on his shirt.

d) (1) His old man would lean against a piling.
(2) His old man would sleep all afternoon.
(3) His mother would sit looking out to sea.

e) (1) He decorated his mother with shells.
(2) He decorated his mother with bright-colored trash.
(3) He found the shells and the trash on the beach.

f) (1) He swam very far out.
(2) The people looked like small dots.
(3) The people were on the beach.

g) (1) Philip played in the shade.
(2) Philip was digging quietly.
(3) Philip was finding things.

h) (1) Ben wanted to stay at the beach.
(2) Ben wanted to be at the beach when everyone had gone home.
(3) Ben wanted to be at the beach when the beach was deserted.

C. SUGGESTIONS FOR WRITING

1. Give your idea of a perfect picnic. Where would it be held? What would you eat?
2. How does a picnic (or a similar informal meal) in your culture

differ from the picnic described in the story? What are some similarities and differences?

3. Long Beach is a popular beach on Long Island, New York. Describe a popular beach or sea resort in your country.

4. Retell the story from Winnie's point of view.

KNOXVILLE: SUMMER 1915

James Agee

James Agee (1909–1955) was an American poet, novelist, and film writer. His most famous works are Let Us Now Praise Famous Men, The Morning Watch, *and* A Death in the Family, *which won the Pulitzer Prize in 1958.*

The following selection is part of "Knoxville: Summer 1915," which is the first section of A Death in the Family. *In his sensitive and poetic style Agee tells, in this novel, how the sudden death of a father affects his family.*

On the rough wet grass of the back yard my father and mother have spread quilts. We all lie there, my mother, my father, my uncle, my aunt, and I too am lying there. First we were sitting up, then one of us lay down, and then we all lay down, on our stomachs, or on our sides, or on our backs, and they have kept on talking. They are not talking much, and the talk is quiet, of nothing in particular, of nothing at all in particular, of nothing at all. The stars are wide and alive, they seem each like a smile of great sweetness, and they seem very near. All my people are larger bodies than mine, quiet, with voices gentle and meaningless like the voices of sleeping birds. One is an artist, he is living at

51

home. One is a musician, she is living at home. One is my mother who is good to me. One is my father who is good to me. By some chance, here they are, all on this earth; and who shall ever tell the sorrow of being on this earth, lying, on quilts, on the grass, in a summer evening, among the sounds of the night. May God bless my people, my uncle, my aunt, my mother, my good father, oh, remember them kindly in their time of trouble; and in the hour of their taking away.

GLOSS

by some chance: accidentally, not planned

who shall ever tell the sorrow of being on this earth: who will be able to describe the sad experience of life on this earth. *Shall* is often used with the third person in legal, religious, and poetic language.

May God bless: I hope that God will bless. This sentence is in the form of a prayer.

in the hour of their taking away: at the time of their deaths

A. COMPREHENSION

1. Where are the narrator and his family?
2. What are they lying on? Why?
3. How many people are there in the back yard?
4. What are they talking about?
5. What time of day is it? How do you know?
6. Do you think the narrator is old or young? How do you know?
7. What kind of voices do the people have?
8. In addition to his mother and father, who lives with the narrator? What are their professions?
9. What does the narrator ask God to do?

B. LANGUAGE EXERCISES

1. VOCABULARY

Fill in the blanks using words from the lists on the next page. Some of the words may be used more than once.

quick   sit
gentle   seem
rough   lie
alive   keep on

It is a _____ summer day, and the waves of

the sea are _____. It is good to be _____.

I want to _____ in my boat and do nothing at all.

If the sea does not become _____, I'll _____

sailing.

bless	grass	sounds	in particular
spread	chance	stars	kindly
lay down	back yard	sorrows	meaningless
took away	quilts	stomachs	

We _____ our blankets on the _____;

we _____ and covered ourselves with _____.

The _____ of the night were quiet and gentle. The

_____ were bright. We talked of nothing _____

_____, and soon we fell asleep.

2. VARYING THE THEME

Imagine that the story was different. What might have
happened?

SITUATION
There were no stars

RESPONSE
The night was dark
        or
The people couldn't see each
    other

SITUATION	*RESPONSE*

The grass wasn't wet
The narrator didn't be-
   lieve in God
It was winter
The house had no back
   yard
The boy had no relatives

3. THE LANGUAGE OF THE POET

Agee writes like a poet. He describes the stars as wide and alive.

a) What other words could you use to describe the stars?
b) What words could you use to describe grass? evening? voices?

4. SOUNDS

a) What kinds of sounds would you hear on a summer evening?
b) What kinds of sounds would you hear on a winter evening?
c) What sounds do you hear in the city?
d) What sounds do you hear in the country?
e) Listen to the words that Carl Sandburg has used to describe
   a city:

> In the evening twilight in the skyscraper office
> And the boom boom of a big steamboat docking
> And the auto horns and the corner newsboys
> Only half heard as far up as sixteen floors . . .

What other sounds would you hear in a big city today?

5. PRAYERS

a) Agee prays that God will bless his family. Here is a common children's prayer in English:

Now I lay me down to sleep
I pray the Lord my soul to keep
If I should die before I wake
I pray the Lord my soul to take.

b) What are some children's prayers that you remember?

6. FAMILY RELATIONSHIPS

a) How do you know that the narrator feels comfortable with his family?
b) In what ways do the families in this selection and in "Like the Lion's Tooth" seem different?
c) Compare the relationship between the narrator and his father in this selection and in "Leaf." In what ways are the fathers similar? In what ways are they different?
d) Describe your relatives the way Agee has.

Example: One is an artist.

7. SENTENCE COMBINING

This is an exercise in combining three short sentences into one longer and better sentence. Your final sentence should have the same ideas as the original sentences, but you may make changes.

Example: (1) The children were delightful.
    (2) The children were rough.
    (3) The children were spoiled.

    The children were delightful, but they were rough and spoiled.

a) (1) My father and mother put quilts on the grass.
    (2) The grass was wet.
    (3) The grass was rough.

b) (1) The stars are wide.
    (2) The stars are alive.
    (3) The stars seem very near.

c) (1) They kept on talking.
   (2) They talked quietly.
   (3) They talked of nothing in particular.
d) (1) He lives at home.
   (2) He lives with his mother.
   (3) His mother is an artist.
e) (1) Their voices are gentle.
   (2) Their voices are meaningless.
   (3) Their voices are like the voices of sleeping birds.

C. SUGGESTIONS FOR WRITING

1. Describe a particular evening with your family.
2. Rewrite the selection with conversations between the mother and father and aunt and uncle.
3. Describe a family that you are familiar with. Are the parents good to their children? What things do they do together?
4. Describe a time when you were comfortable or uncomfortable with your family.

THE GOOD OLD DAYS

William Carlos Williams

William Carlos Williams (1883–1963) was an American doctor who wrote both prose and poetry. Good examples of his poetry can be found in his book Selected Poems. *In much of his prose, he wrote about American attitudes.*

"The Good Old Days" is a chapter in his book The Farmers' Daughters, *a collection of stories published in 1961. Notice that the author does not use quotation marks when he writes conversation.*

In 1910 I was one of a number of passengers going along the Grand Canal in a gondola toward the Venice railway terminal. We had only a minute or two in which to catch the train as suitcase in hand, I tore up the steps, swung through the waiting room, bought my ticket and made for the gate. As I went through, hot under the collar and breathing fast, a guard stopped me.

Piano! Piano! he said in a quiet voice. *E sempre tempo in Italia!* That may not be Italian but that's the way I remember it. Easy! Easy! There's always time in Italy! He was right. I had plenty of time in which to make that train.

It was a lovely country. Yes, and when my brother went over during the first war to take up his duties with the Red Cross it was much the same.

He tells how, when the Americans arrived and the Italian units were turning over their offices and equipment to us, there was a big, formal to-do. It wasn't so big perhaps as it was formal and, in a sense, not too formal at that. Anyhow they made an affair of it, in true Italian style.

The Americans, naturally, had the cash and all that. There was plenty of work to do too so they started in under Colonel Davidson in true big-business style. Everything in the old offices was cleaned out. Modern equipment was moved in—it had all been brought along from New York.

There were half a dozen typewriters, all sparkling new, desks, chairs, filing cabinets, cards, stationery, boxes of ribbons, carbon paper by the bale, everything. And assistants and girls to go with them. It was impressive and the old Italian force was impressed. They thought it was wonderful.

No wonder Americans go places. You can see it right away. A great people, a great nation! Business geniuses. The American staff was rather proud of it themselves.

Well sir, when everything was set up they had this little affair that I mentioned. Colonel Davidson spoke in English and my brother translated for him. A few messages and telegrams were read and transmitted then, last of all, the old boy who had been at the head of the Italian office before the Americans moved in stood up to make a final gesture. In his hands he held a heavy, round stone.

As he talked all eyes were on the stone.

After a few preliminary remarks he turned to Colonel Davidson and said, I have been greatly impressed by your American efficiency. But there is one thing I should like to present to you, one reminder of the old Italian spirit, part of our own past equipment, which I beg you to keep and to use for what it is worth.

Everybody wondered what the hell he was going to say next.

You see this stone. This is for your corre-
spondence. When letters come into the office you
will place them in a neat pile and lay this stone upon
them. You do not disturb them then for two weeks.
At the end of that time you will begin to take away
the letters, one at a time, from the bottom of the
pile, five or six letters every day. And you will find,
if you do this, that most of them have answered
themselves when they are opened. It is a very
efficient system and saves much labor.

GLOSS

Grand Canal: the main canal in Venice
catch the train: get to the train
tore up the steps: ran up the steps
swung through: hurried through
made for: went toward
hot under the collar: excited
make that train: get to that train
went over: went to Europe from the United States
the first war: World War I (1914–1918)
turning over: giving
to-do: ceremony
ribbons: typewriter ribbons
No wonder Americans go places: it is not surprising that Americans
    accomplish a lot
Well sir: Well, sir; the author writes as if he were talking to a
    particular person and instead of the person's name he uses the
    word *sir*
set up: arranged
the old boy: a phrase, often affectionate, for a male boss or head of
    a group
what the hell: very informal; used here to indicate emphasis

A. COMPREHENSION

1. Where was the narrator in 1910?
2. Why was he hurrying?

3. What did the guard say to him?
4. Did the narrator catch the train?
5. Why did the narrator's brother go to Italy?
6. Why did the Italians have a ceremony?
7. What had the Americans brought from New York?
8. What did the Italians think of the new American things?
9. What did the head of the Italian office give to the Americans?
10. What did the Italian advise the Americans to do with the stone and the letters?
11. How long did he tell them to leave the letters in the pile?
12. Why was the system efficient?
13. What do you think the title means?

B. LANGUAGE EXERCISES

1. VOCABULARY

Fill in the blanks using the words listed below. Then look at the first two paragraphs of the selection to see how well you did.

passengers	fast	set up	begged
brothers	greatly	stop	catch
staff	right	make	on
quiet	formal	remember	toward
heavy	proud	bought	

In 1910 I was one of a number of _____

going along the Grand Canal in a gondola _____

the Venice railway terminal. We had only a minute or

two in which to _____ the train as suitcase in

hand, I tore up the steps, swung through the waiting room,

_____ my ticket and made for the gate. As I went

through, hot under the collar and breathing _____,

a guard stopped me.

Piano! Piano! he said in a _____ voice. *E sempre tempo in Italia!* That may not be Italian, but that's the way I _____ it. Easy! Easy! There's always time in Italy. He was _____. I had plenty of time in which to _____ that train.

2. CONNECTING IDEAS

The following sentences are not in a normal order. Arrange them in an order that shows how the ideas are connected. You may connect sentences if you want to.

a) Take the letters away from the bottom of the pile.
b) Put a stone on the pile.
c) That will save you much labor.
d) Many of the letters will not need an answer.
e) Then take away the letters one at a time.
f) Letters come into the office.
g) Don't disturb the pile for two weeks.
h) Put them into a pile.

3. TRUE OR FALSE

Tell whether the following statements are True (T) or False (F) or Not Mentioned (N) in the story you have just read. If a statement is not true, change it so that it is true according to the story.

a) At the beginning the narrator was in a boat.
b) The narrator left his suitcase in the waiting room.
c) The narrator's brother worked with the Red Cross.
d) The Americans used the office equipment which was left by the Italians.
e) The Italians in the office were not impressed by the Americans.

f) The brother of the narrator spoke Italian.
g) The Americans brought the stone as a present.
h) The Italians had a system for answering letters.
i) The Red Cross office was near Venice.

4. THINGS

Williams lists the objects necessary for an office at the time of World War I.

a) What other objects would be necessary for an office today?
b) List the objects necessary for an activity or place that interests you: for example, a dentist's office; an automobile repair shop; a bookstore; collecting stamps.

5. IN THE OLD DAYS

Some people call the old days "the good old days." Other people think that the old days were not very good.

a) In a few sentences, compare one aspect of life as it was in your culture in the old days and as it is now.

Example: Twenty years ago students often wore jackets and ties to school. Today many students wear blue jeans and open shirts.

b) Do you think the old days were better than now or not?
 (1) How was it better in the old days?
 (2) How was it worse in the old days?
c) How do you think Williams would have answered 5(b)?

6. CULTURAL DIFFERENCES

Williams writes of a difference between Americans and Italians.

a) Note a difference between your culture and another culture. You might consider differences in food, clothing, entertainment, education, public behavior, attitudes toward sex, etc.

Example: For food, you might answer such questions as:

How much food is eaten at each meal?
What are the basic foods?
Do men and women eat the same kinds of food?
With what utensils is food eaten?
What foods are given to babies?
What foods are given to people when they are sick?

b) People in different cultures have different attitudes toward time. How important is it to you to be on time when you
   (1) go to school
   (2) go to church
   (3) go to work
   (4) leave work
   (5) meet a friend
   (6) catch a train

c) People have written that Americans like fast cars, alcohol, new things, cleanliness, privacy, and bigness. Others add that the most important things for Americans are duty and work.
   (1) From your knowledge of Americans, do you agree or disagree with the characteristics described above?
   (2) What kind of list would you make for people in your culture?

7. SENTENCE COMBINING

This is an exercise in combining three short sentences into one longer and better sentence. Your final sentence should have the same ideas as the original sentences, but you may make changes.

Example: (1) The children were delightful.
            (2) The children were rough.
            (3) The children were spoiled.

The children were delightful, but they were rough
and spoiled.

a) (1) It was in 1910.
   (2) I was in a gondola.
   (3) The gondola was going toward the Venice railway
       terminal.

b) (1) I ran up the steps.
   (2) I bought my ticket.
   (3) I hurried to the gate.

c) (1) I was walking through the gate.
   (2) I was breathing fast.
   (3) A guard stopped me.

d) (1) My brother went to Italy.
   (2) It was a lovely country.
   (3) It still is.

e) (1) My brother went to Italy.
   (2) My brother went during the first war.
   (3) My brother went to work for the Red Cross.

f) (1) He arrived in Italy.
   (2) He spoke only English.
   (3) I translated for him.

g) (1) He talked to the group.
   (2) Everyone in the group was looking at the stone.
   (3) The stone was heavy and round.

h) (1) Your American efficiency is impressive.
   (2) I would like to give you a present.
   (3) The present is a reminder of Italian efficiency.

i) (1) Letters come into this office.
   (2) Place the letters in a neat pile.
   (3) Put this stone on the letters.

j) (1) Put the letters in a pile.
   (2) Put a stone on the letters.
   (3) Do not disturb the letters for two weeks.

k) (1) It is an efficient system.
   (2) It is an Italian system.
   (3) It saves much labor.

C. SUGGESTIONS FOR WRITING

1. Describe a way of doing something that is characteristic of your culture.
2. People say that the French are gourmets, the Americans want to make money, the Japanese work very hard, etc. Agree or disagree with one generalization about people from another culture.
3. Agree or disagree with the statement "People are the same everywhere."
4. Describe one change that has taken place in the last twenty-five years in education, architecture, transportation, or clothing.

THE VIVISECTOR

Patrick White

Patrick White (b. 1912) is an Australian novelist who won the Nobel Prize for literature in 1973. Among his best-known novels are The Tree of Man *and* Riders in the Chariot. *He has also written short stories and plays.*

In this selection from White's novel The Vivisector, *it is six-year-old Hurtle Duffield's first day of school. Miss Adams is his teacher.*

"What are you doing, Hurtle Duffield?" Miss Adams had smelled a rat.

Everyone looking.

"Droring," he confessed, though it pained him to do so.

It pained Miss Adams equally. He had to take it up to her. The girl with the flossy fringe giggled.

"What is it supposed to be?" Miss Adams squinted and asked through her cold.

"Death," he said and heard his own voice.

"Death?" Miss Adams was frowning. "Looks like a kind of elephant to me. An elephant with hair instead of hide."

"It is," he said. "An elephant in a lion's skin."

"But Death? An elephant is such a gentle creature. Large, but gentle."

"Not always it isn't," he corrected. "It can

trample its keeper, without any warning, and rip
with its tusks."

All the kids were interested. Some of them
pretended to be afraid. Perhaps some of them were.

Miss Adams made a noise through her blocked
nose. "You were supposed to be forming pothooks."

"Pothooks! I can write!"

"You sound like a vain boy. At your age. I
don't like know-alls. Who was your teacher?"

"I learned myself, I suppose. At first. Then
Mr. Olliphant showed me some of the finer points."

Nobody else was making a sound.

"Mr. Olliphant?" She was so ignorant she
hadn't even heard of the rector.

"Seeing that you can write," Miss Adams said,
"you will write me something, Hurtle. Something
about yourself. Your home. Your life. A
composition, in fact. If, as you claim, you are so
advanced."

She made a sour, thin smile as she screwed up
the drawing of Death and lobbed it into the basket.

He was glad to return to his bench. He would
never write if he could draw, but he was so sick
of school, it would be a relief to tell about himself.

GLOSS

smelled a rat: thought that something wrong was being done
Everyone looking: Everyone was looking
droring: drawing; the author has spelled the word the way he thinks
    Hurtle pronounced it
to do so: to do that; that is, to confess
with the flossy fringe: with shiny hair over her forehead
asked through her cold: Miss Adams's voice sounded strange
    because she had a cold
kids: children, colloquial usage
pothooks: curved strokes made by children who are learning
    to write
know-alls: people who think they know everything

finer: more complex
screwed up: twisted into a ball
lobbed: threw
sick of: unhappy with

A. COMPREHENSION

1. What was Hurtle Duffield doing?
2. What did the girl with the flossy fringe do?
3. What was the drawing supposed to be?
4. What did the drawing look like to Miss Adams?
5. Does Miss Adams think that an elephant is a gentle creature?
6. Does Hurtle think that an elephant is a gentle creature?
7. What did some of the children do?
8. What was Hurtle supposed to be doing?
9. Why didn't he want to form pothooks?
10. Who taught Hurtle to write?
11. Who was Mr. Olliphant? What did he teach Hurtle?
12. What did Miss Adams ask Hurtle to write?
13. What did Miss Adams do with the drawing of Death?
14. Which did Hurtle prefer: drawing or writing?
15. Why was it a relief for Hurtle to tell about himself?

B. LANGUAGE EXERCISES

1. VOCABULARY

Fill in the blanks using words from the list below. Some of the words may be used more than once.

pretended	supposed	vain	creature
frowned	interested	glad	elephant
claimed	gentle	sick	drawings
giggled	afraid	ignorant	relief

"All the _____ are _____ to be on

the wall," the teacher said. The girl with the flossy fringe

_____. Hurtle _____ not to hear the

teacher. The teacher looked at Hurtle and _____.

"Why isn't your drawing on the wall, Hurtle?" she asked.

Hurtle was _____ to put his drawing on the wall;

he had drawn an _____ with his teacher's head.

At that moment the bell rang. Hurtle was _____.

He was so _____ of school that it would be a

_____ to leave.

2. CONNECTING IDEAS

The following sentences are not in a normal order. Arrange them in an order which shows how the ideas are connected. You can combine sentences. There may be more than one possible order.

a) Miss Adams said it looked like an elephant.
b) "It can trample its keeper and rip with its tusks."
c) Hurtle made a drawing of Death.
d) "Not always," he said.
e) She took the drawing and threw it into the basket.
f) He showed the drawing to Miss Adams.
g) "But an elephant is a gentle creature," she said.
h) Hurtle said it was an elephant.

3. TRUE OR FALSE

Tell whether the following statements are True (T) or False (F) or Not Mentioned (N) in the story you have just read. If a statement is not true, change it so that it is true according to the story.

a) Hurtle Duffield was a teacher.
b) Miss Adams was afraid of rats.

c) Miss Adams had a cold.

d) Hurtle liked the girl with the flossy fringe.

e) Miss Adams thought elephants were not gentle.

f) Some of the other children were drawing, too.

g) Miss Adams knew who Mr. Olliphant was.

h) Mr. Olliphant helped Hurtle learn to write.

i) Miss Adams planned to show Hurtle's drawing to the rector.

j) Hurtle liked to write more than he liked to draw.

4. SCHOOL

a) What kinds of things did you have to do in elementary school? In secondary school?

b) What were your favorite subjects or activities?

c) What subjects didn't you like?

d) What should school be like? Is it like that?

5. TELLING ABOUT YOURSELF

a) If you had to describe yourself using only five adjectives, which adjectives would you choose?

b) Which five adjectives would you choose to describe a classmate, a relative, an enemy?

c) If you had to describe the five most important events in your life, which ones would you choose?

6. SENTENCE COMBINING

This is an exercise in combining three short sentences into one longer and better sentence. Your final sentence should have the same ideas as the original sentences, but you may make changes.

Example: (1) The children were delightful.
(2) The children were rough.
(3) The children were spoiled.

The children were delightful, but they were rough and spoiled.

a) (1) Hurtle confessed.
   (2) Hurtle said that he was drawing.
   (3) It pained Hurtle to say that he was drawing.

b) (1) An elephant is usually a gentle creature.
   (2) An elephant can trample its keeper.
   (3) An elephant can rip with its tusks.

c) (1) All the kids were interested.
   (2) Some of the kids pretended to be afraid.
   (3) Perhaps some of the kids were afraid.

d) (1) She was very ignorant.
   (2) She hadn't heard of the rector.
   (3) The rector's name was Mr. Olliphant.

e) (1) He was glad to return to his bench.
   (2) He could write.
   (3) He could tell about himself.

f) (1) The teacher was very angry.
   (2) The teacher took the drawing.
   (3) The teacher threw the drawing into the wastebasket.

C. SUGGESTIONS FOR WRITING

1. Describe your first day of school.
2. Compare the personalities of two very different teachers whom you had.
3. Describe an experience in school that was embarrassing for you.
4. Write a brief autobiography.

DEATH

SPEAKS

W. Somerset Maugham

---

*Somerset Maugham (1874–1965) was a writer of
stories, novels, and plays. His works are always
entertaining, and they have become popular throughout
the world. See his* Collected Short Stories *(1951) and*
Collected Plays *(1931).*

The following story comes from his play Sheppey.
*The story begins in the same way as many popular
folk and children stories: "There was a . . . ." or
"Once there was . . . ." Some of the language is
old-fashioned: the use of* provisions *for food, for
example. Some of the language is more formal than
usual: "I will avoid . . . my fate." The author also has
not put in punctuation marks where we would expect
them.*

*The title "Death Speaks" means that Death, who
is a woman here, is telling the story. The words* I
and me *refer to Death.*

There was a merchant in Bagdad who sent his
servant to market to buy provisions and in a little
while the servant came back, white and trembling,
and said, Master, just now when I was in the
market-place I was jostled by a woman in the crowd
and when I turned I saw it was Death that jostled
me. She looked at me and made a threatening
gesture; now, lend me your horse, and I will ride
away from this city and avoid my fate. I will go to

Samarra and there Death will not find me. The
merchant lent him his horse, and the servant
mounted it, and he dug his spurs in its flanks and as
fast as the horse could gallop he went. Then the
merchant went down to the market-place and he
saw me standing in the crowd and he came to me
and said, Why did you make a threatening gesture
to my servant when you saw him this morning?
That was not a threatening gesture, I said, it was
only a start of surprise. I was astonished to see him
in Bagdad, for I had an appointment with him
tonight in Samarra.

GLOSS

Bagdad: capital of Iraq
to market: to the market
Master: a form of address that was used by servants
Samarra: a town in Iraq, about 65 miles northwest of Bagdad
start: here, a noun meaning a sudden movement

A. COMPREHENSION

1. Who went to the market?
2. Why did he go?
3. How did the servant look when he came back?
4. What did a woman in the crowd do?
5. Who was the woman?
6. What kind of gesture did the woman make?
7. What did the servant ask the master?
8. Why did the servant want to leave the city?
9. Why did he want to go to Samarra?
10. Did the merchant help the servant? How?
11. Where did the merchant go?
12. Whom did he see in the crowd?
13. What did he say to Death?
14. Did Death say she had made a threatening gesture?
15. Why was Death surprised?
16. Who was the narrator of the story?

B. LANGUAGE EXERCISES

1. VOCABULARY

Fill in the blanks using words from the list below. Some of the words may be used more than once.

surprise	appointment	trembling
gesture	astonished	avoid
crowd	threatening	in a little while

_____ the servant will arrive in Samarra. He will probably walk through the market-place. Someone in the _____ will make a _____. The gesture will mean, "Come here."

The servant went to Samarra to _____ Death, but, to his _____, he will find Death there.

His _____ with Death was not in Bagdad but in Samarra. The servant will be _____.

2. CONNECTING IDEAS

The following sentences are not in a normal order. Arrange them in an order that shows how the ideas are connected. You can connect sentences if you think it will be better.

a) He told the merchant that a woman had pushed him.
b) He had a servant.
c) The servant came back soon.
d) A merchant lived in Bagdad.
e) He sent the servant to the market.
f) He said that the woman was Death.
g) He wanted the servant to get some food.

3. TRUE OR FALSE

Tell whether the following statements are True (T) or False (F) or Not Mentioned (N) in the story you have just read. If a statement is not true, change it so that it is true according to the story.

a) The merchant lived in Bagdad.
b) The servant understood the gesture of Death.
c) The servant was not afraid of Death.
d) The servant had his own horse.
e) The servant went to Samarra.
f) The merchant followed the servant to Samarra.
g) Death had a home in Samarra.
h) Death rode on a white horse.

4. FATE

Many people throughout the world believe in fate.

a) There are many sayings in English that show a belief in fate. For example:
   (1) When it's your time to go, it's your time to go.
   (2) That's life.
   (3) You have to take the bitter with the sweet.
   Are there similar sayings in your culture?
b) Are there people in your culture who believe in fate? Are there any stories or songs that illustrate this belief?

5. VARYING THE THEME

a) Imagine that the story was different. What might have happened?

SITUATION	RESPONSE
The merchant wasn't hungry.	He didn't send his servant to the market-place.

SITUATION	RESPONSE
The merchant didn't have a horse.	
There was no crowd in the market-place.	
The servant was blind.	
The servant wasn't afraid of death.	
The merchant was afraid of death.	

b) One possible ending for the story is given in the vocabulary exercise. Can you think of other possible endings?

6. PERSONIFICATION

a) Death is a woman in this story but usually Death does not appear as a person in contemporary English writing. How does Death appear in your culture?

b) In many languages, people and objects are considered masculine, feminine, or neuter (sometimes these are just names for different grammatical forms). For example, in English a ship has usually been considered feminine. If your language uses masculine and feminine markings, what are the following usually considered?

moon	doctor	engineer	teacher
sea	radio	team	computer
car	earth		

7. GESTURES

Death makes a threatening gesture to the servant.

a) What kind of a gesture do you think Death made?
b) How would you make a threatening gesture?

c) What gestures would you use for:

(1) Hello.
(2) Goodbye.
(3) Come here.
(4) It's wonderful.
(5) I don't know.
(6) What did you say?

(7) I've made a mistake.
(8) It's hot.
(9) It's cold.
(10) Good luck!
(11) He's crazy.
(12) I don't believe it!

8. SENTENCE COMBINING

This is an exercise in combining three short sentences into one longer and better sentence. Your final sentence should have the same ideas as the original sentences, but you may make changes.

Example:

(1) The children were delightful.
(2) The children were rough.
(3) The children were spoiled.

The children were delightful, but they were rough and spoiled.

a) (1) The servant came back in a little while.
   (2) The servant was white.
   (3) The servant was trembling.

b) (1) I was in the market.
   (2) I was jostled by a woman.
   (3) The woman made a threatening gesture.

c) (1) Lend me your horse.
   (2) I will ride away from this city.
   (3) I will avoid my fate.

d) (1) The servant mounted the horse.
   (2) The servant dug his spurs in the flanks of the horse.
   (3) The servant went as fast as he could.

e) (1) I was astonished to see him there.
   (2) I had an appointment with him.
   (3) I had an appointment in another city.

C. SUGGESTIONS FOR WRITING

1. Retell the story. Imagine that it takes place today in a big city.
2. Describe an incident in which someone escaped death.
3. Describe a situation in which gestures were important.
4. Describe a situation in which not knowing gestures has led or can lead to a problem in communication.

THE RETURN

Gayl Jones

Gayl Jones (b. 1949) was born in Lexington, Kentucky. She is now a graduate student at Brown University, from which she will receive her doctorate in creative writing in 1975. She has had her poems and short stories published in Essence *and* Panache. *Her forthcoming novel,* Corregidora, *will be published by Random House.*

In "The Return," Jones writes about the lives of three black students at an American college today— their interests and enthusiasms.

Joseph and my brother Steven were loners the first year of college. They met the second year and liked each other and started going around together. Steven would invade Joseph's room and they would read books aloud and discuss things. Steven was tall with long feet. His favorite saint was St. Martin Perez, the black Peruvian, and his favorite writer was Kafka—after he had outgrown Joyce's *Portrait of the Artist As a Young Man.* He had never gotten through *Ulysses.* Joseph was two or three inches shorter than Steven, about five foot ten. He had been a follower of Mohammed and before that Jesus, and was a journalism major at a Midwestern college before he came East and got interested in religion. He had a mustache and Steven said he still wore a belly band just because he liked the feel of it. He was thin and went in for Yogi. He was serious

in his pursuit of the mysteries, and had learned
to do many things with his mind and body, Steven
said. Steven was unofficially majoring in everything.

I met Joseph shortly after Steven did. I went
into the snack shop one afternoon, and Steven was
sitting with a young man who wore dark pants
and a gray sweater. His hair grew high on his
forehead and he had large dark eyes, and a half-
smile. He had a beard in those days. I went over
to say hello to Steven. When he didn't introduce us,
I said, "I'm Dora, Steven's sister."

"Joseph Corey," he answered, but neither he
nor Steven said anything else to me, so I left. Joseph
Corey would call on me sometimes and we would
go out together, but hardly ever would the three
of us be together. When Steven and Joseph were
together, I felt my entrances intrusions, and Steven
seemed to feel that way too. Even Joseph could
be cold at these times. So I had learned to simply
wave and go my way.

GLOSS

loners: people who do not have many friends
going around together: doing things together
gotten through: finished reading
Ulysses: a long, difficult novel by the Irish writer James Joyce
a journalism major: a student who specializes in journalism
went in for Yogi: became very interested in Yoga
the mysteries: mysterious subjects such as ancient and secret
    religions
call on: visit
wave: wave my hand
go my way: leave

A. COMPREHENSION

1. Did Joseph and Steven have a lot of friends the first year of
    college?
2. When did they meet?

3. What would they do together?
4. What did Steven look like?
5. Who was his favorite author?
6. What did Joseph look like?
7. What did he do before he came East?
8. What was Steven majoring in?
9. What was he interested in now?
10. Where did the narrator meet Joseph?
11. What was Joseph wearing?
12. Did Steven introduce Dora to Joseph?
13. Why did Dora leave the snack shop?
14. Did Joseph, Steve, and Dora go out together?
15. What did Dora usually do when she met Steven and Joseph together?

B. LANGUAGE EXERCISES

1. VOCABULARY

Fill in the blanks using words and phrases listed below. Some of the words may be used more than once.

met	discuss	interested
go out	gotten through	together
call on	favorite	major
going around	serious	followers
went in for		

I remember the first time I _____ Henry.

He was a _____ student who was very _____

_____ in philosophy. That wasn't my _____ sub-

ject, but at least I was able to _____ it with him.

Soon he started to _____ me, and we would often

_____ to movies and to dances. We enjoyed being

_____ until he started _____ with the

_____ of a secret religion.

2. CONNECTING IDEAS

The following sentences are not in a normal order. Arrange them in an order that shows how the ideas are connected. You may connect the sentences if you want to.

a) I sat down.
b) I went into the snack shop.
c) It was a corner table.
d) So I left.
e) They said nothing to me.
f) I got a glass of milk.
g) They were talking.
h) I went over to their table.

3. VARYING THE THEME

Imagine that the story was different. What might have happened?

SITUATION	RESPONSE
Joseph stayed at the mid-western college.	He didn't meet Steven and Dora.
Steven introduced Dora to Joseph.	
Joseph and Steven had a lot of friends.	
Steven and Joseph liked music.	
Steven and Joseph wanted Dora to be with them.	
Joseph was not very serious.	
Joseph never called on Dora.	
Joseph was fat.	

4. INTERESTS

Joseph and Steven would read books aloud and discuss things.

a) What kinds of things would they discuss?
b) What kinds of things do college students in your country discuss?
c) What kinds of things do you think are discussed by: telephone operators, deep sea divers, weather forecasters, athletes?

5. STUDENT LIFE

a) Where do college students in your country spend their free time?
b) How do college students dress in your country? In other countries?
c) A student at an American university usually majors in a subject by the third or fourth year. When do students in your country choose a major?
d) For what reasons do students go to universities?

6. SENTENCE COMBINING

This is an exercise in combining three short sentences into one longer and better sentence. Your final sentence should have the same ideas as the original sentences, but you may make changes.

Example: (1) The children were delightful.
(2) The children were rough.
(3) The children were spoiled.

The children were delightful, but they were rough and spoiled.

a) (1) They met during the second year of college.
(2) They liked each other.
(3) They started going around together.

b) (1) First he was a journalism major in a midwestern college.
   (2) Then he came East.
   (3) Then he became interested in religion.

c) (1) My brother was tall.
   (2) His friend was a little shorter.
   (3) They both had long beards.

d) (1) My brother was unofficially majoring in everything.
   (2) My brother liked to spend a lot of time sitting in snack shops.
   (3) My brother liked to discuss things.

e) (1) I went into the snack shop one afternoon.
   (2) My brother was sitting with a young man.
   (3) The young man was wearing dark pants.

f) (1) My brother didn't say anything to me.
   (2) The young man didn't say anything to me.
   (3) I left.

g) (1) He called on me sometimes.
   (2) We would go out together.
   (3) My brother hardly ever came with us.

C. SUGGESTIONS FOR WRITING

1. Compare two good friends. Do they like the same things?
2. Observe someone carefully and describe what he or she looks like.
3. Observe a meeting between two people and describe what happens. What gestures do they use?
4. Describe ways of greeting people in your culture and compare them to ways of greeting people in another culture that you know.

THE MAN WITH THE DOG

R. Prawer Jhabvala

R. Prawer Jhabvala (b. 1927) is a contemporary writer
of short stories and sketches. Born in Germany, she
has lived most of her life in India, and she writes about
life in that country.

The following selection comes from a book
entitled A Stronger Climate, a collection of short stories
about Europeans who are living in India and who are
having difficulty in adjusting to life there. The title
means that the climate (not just the weather but also the
way of life) of India is a stronger climate than the
Europeans are used to.

In this passage from a story called "The Man with
the Dog," an Indian woman thinks about how her life
has changed.

It is strange how often in one lifetime one
changes and changes again, even an ordinary
person like myself. When I look back, I see myself
first as the young girl in my father's house,
impatient, waiting for things to happen; then as the
calm wife and mother, fulfilling all my many
duties; and then again, when [the] children are
bigger and my dear husband, many years older than
myself, has moved far away from me and I am

more his daughter than his wife—then again I am different. In those years we mostly lived in the hills, and I would go for long walks by myself, for hours and hours, sometimes with great happiness to be there among those great green mountains in sun and mist. But sometimes also I was full of misery and longed for something as great and beautiful as those mountains to fill my own life which seemed, in those years, very empty. But when my dear husband left us for ever, I came down from the mountains and then began that fashionable town life of which I have already spoken. But that too has finished. Now I get up in the mornings, I drink my tea, I walk round the garden with a peaceful heart; I pick a handful of blossoms; and these I lay at the feet of Vishnu in my prayer-room. Without taking my bath or changing out of the old cotton sari in which I have spent the night, I sit for many hours on the veranda, doing nothing, only looking out at the flowers and the birds. My thoughts come and go.

GLOSS

has moved far away from me: here, this means *has become very different from me*
longed for: wanted
left us for ever: died
fashionable town life: the kind of life a wealthy woman living in a city would have
Vishnu: a god in Hindu theology
sari: a long dress worn by Hindu women
spent: refers to time

A. COMPREHENSION

1. What does the narrator think is strange?
2. Describe the narrator as a girl in her father's house.
3. Describe the narrator as a wife.

4. Where did the narrator and her family live?
5. What kind of walks did the narrator take?
6. How did the narrator feel sometimes?
7. When did the narrator come down from the mountains?
8. What kind of life did she then have?
9. Does she still have the same kind of life?
10. How does she spend her mornings now?
11. What does she do on the veranda?

B. LANGUAGE EXERCISES

1. VOCABULARY

Fill in the blanks using words from the list below. Some of the words may be used more than once.

peaceful	strange	spend
different	fulfilling	change
ordinary	empty	

People have _____ points of view. Something

which seems _____ to one person may seem

_____ to another. A life that seems _____

to one man may seem _____ to another. And

ideas _____ in time. Children often think that

their parents have _____ lives, but, when these

children grow up, they often _____ their time

in the same way as their parents.

2. CONNECTING IDEAS

The following sentences are not in a normal order. Arrange them in an order that shows how the ideas are connected. You can

combine sentences and add connectives if you think it will be
better.

a) But often I longed for my mountains.
b) Now it makes no difference where I live.
c) When I was young we lived in the country.
d) That made me happy because I liked the busy streets.
e) At that time I walked a lot among the mountains.
f) Then we moved to the city.

3. TRUE OR FALSE

Tell whether the following statements are True (T) or False
(F) or Not Mentioned (N) in the story you have just read. If a
statement is not true, change it so that it is true according to the
story.

a) People don't change very much.
b) The narrator was always a calm, patient person.
c) The narrator didn't like to be alone.
d) The narrator does not think that she is an ordinary person.
e) The narrator and her husband were the same age.
f) The narrator often went for long walks by herself.
g) The narrator had many sisters in her family.
h) The narrator lived in both the mountains and the city.
i) The narrator was a cousin of her husband.
j) The narrator's husband is dead.
k) The narrator lives in a warm climate.

4. THINKING ABOUT OURSELVES AND OTHERS

The narrator mentions several changes that have taken place
during her lifetime.

a) What does the narrator think about herself during the different periods of her life?
b) What are adjectives that you would use to describe yourself
or someone you know as:
(1) a young girl or boy

(2) a wife or husband
(3) a mother or father
(4) an older man or older woman
c) Describe some activities that are characteristic of a particular person.

Example: My father always has tea in the morning.

5. DESCRIBE IT

The following words are used in this selection:

ordinary   impatient   calm   peaceful   great   beautiful

For each word think of a situation that the word describes.

Example: *exciting:* a trip on a river in a canoe
difficult: adjusting to life in a new place

6. SPENDING TIME

How do you spend your time when you are by yourself?

7. DUTIES

We often think that we have to do certain things. We call these things *duties*.

a) What do you think the narrator's duties were as a wife and mother?
b) What duties do you think are important for a mother? a husband? a teacher? a son?
Do you think your parents (or children) would agree with you?
c) Duties seem to be changing. Women are doing things which they have not done before. Men are also doing things which they have not done before.
(1) What are some examples of these changes?
(2) What are some changes in duties that you would like to see?

8. SENTENCE COMBINING

This is an exercise in combining three short sentences into one longer and better sentence. Your final sentence should have the same ideas as the original sentences, but you may make changes.

Example: (1) The children were delightful.
(2) The children were rough.
(3) The children were spoiled.

The children were delightful, but they were rough and spoiled.

a) (1) I was a young girl in my father's house.
(2) I was impatient.
(3) I was waiting for things to happen.

b) (1) I was calm.
(2) I was a wife.
(3) I was a mother.

c) (1) We lived in the hills.
(2) I would go for long walks.
(3) I would go for hours and hours.

d) (1) My husband died.
(2) I came down from the hills.
(3) I began life in town.

e) (1) I get up in the morning.
(2) I drink my tea.
(3) I walk around the garden.

f) (1) I don't take a bath.
(2) I don't change out of my sari.
(3) I sit for hours on the veranda.

C. SUGGESTIONS FOR WRITING

1. Describe an earlier period in your life.
2. Describe a typical part of your day.
3. Describe an event that changed your life or the life of someone you know.

THE EDIBLE WOMAN

Margaret Atwood

Margaret Atwood (b. 1939) is a Canadian writer. She has published several collections of poetry among which are Procedures for Underground *and* The Animals in That Country. *She is also an ardent canoeist.*

The Edible Woman *is Atwood's first novel. It is set in Toronto. The main idea of the novel is that women are considered as things that can be bought and sold. The title of the novel refers to a sponge cake that is made in the shape of a woman.*

The characters in the selection below are: Joe, a university professor; Clara, Joe's wife; Marian, a friend of Joe's and Clara's. Joe and Marian are at a party talking about Clara. Clara studied at a university and now she is a housewife.

Both of them turned their eyes toward Clara, who was over at the sofa-side of the room, talking with one of the soapwives.

"I worry about her a lot, you know," Joe continued. "I think it's a lot harder for her than for most other women; I think it's harder for any woman who's been to university. She gets the idea she has a mind, her professors pay attention to what she has to say, they treat her like a thinking human being; when she gets married, her core gets invaded. . . ."

"Her what?" Marian asked.

"Her core. The centre of her personality, the thing she's built up; her image of herself, if you like."

"Oh. Yes," said Marian.

"Her feminine role and her core are really in opposition, her feminine role demands passivity from her. . . ."

Marian had a fleeting vision of a large globular pastry, decorated with whipped cream and maraschino cherries, floating suspended in the air above Joe's head.

"So she allows her core to get taken over by the husband. And when the kids come, she wakes up one morning and discovers she doesn't have anything left inside, she's hollow, she doesn't know who she is any more; her core has been destroyed." He shook his head gently and sipped at his drink. "I can see it happening with my own female students. But it would be futile to warn them."

GLOSS

the sofa-side of the room: the part of the room where a sofa was

soapwives: the author has created this word to refer to some women whose husbands are businessmen; one of them manufactures soap

to university: to the university, in American English

centre: center, in American English

get taken over: be dominated

the kids come: she has children

A. COMPREHENSION

1. Where was Clara?
2. What was Clara doing?
3. Who worried about Clara?
4. Why were things harder for Clara?

5. What happens to women who go to the university?
6. How do professors treat women who go to the university?
7. What happens to a university woman when she gets married?
8. What was Marian thinking of while Joe was talking?
9. What happens to a married woman after she has children?
10. Why doesn't Joe warn his female students?

B. LANGUAGE EXERCISES

1. VOCABULARY

Fill in the blanks using words from the list below. Some of the words may be used more than once.

allow	pay attention to	personality
discover	worrying	mind
warn	role	vision
treated	sofa	passivity

After dinner, we sat on the _____. I didn't

_____ what Joe was saying. I was _____

about Clara. She looked unhappy. At the university, she

had had a strong _____. She had had a good

_____. Her professors had _____ her well.

It was hard for her to adjust to a feminine _____.

2. CONNECTING IDEAS

The following sentences are not in a normal order. Arrange them in an order that shows how the ideas are connected. You can combine sentences. There may be more than one possible order.

a) They treat her like a thinking person.
b) She allows her husband to take over.
c) Marian goes to the university.

d) She forgets that she has a mind.
e) She has children.
f) The professors tell her that she has a mind.
g) Then she gets married.

3. WARNINGS

a) What would Joe say if he were warning his students?

Example: If you get married, you will _____.
Don't _____.

b) Suppose you are one of Joe's students and he tries to warn you. What will you reply?

4. EDUCATION

a) What kinds of people go to a university in your culture?
b) What do you think the role of the university should be in your culture?
   1) Should universities be primarily professional schools?
   2) Should universities offer practical training?
   3) Should universities be centers for adult education?

5. WOMEN

a) What is the image of women in your culture?
b) Describe the possibilities for women to work in your culture. Do all women work? Which women work? Which jobs are available to women? Do men and women get equal pay?
c) What changes do you think should take place in the role of women in your culture?

6. HUSBAND-WIFE ROLES

a) What responsibilities does a wife have in your culture?
b) What responsibilities does a husband have in your culture?

c) Are the responsibilities of husbands and wives changing now? In what ways?

7. SENTENCE COMBINING

This is an exercise in combining three short sentences into one longer and better sentence. Your final sentence should have the same ideas as the original sentences, but you may make changes.

Example:　(1) The children were delightful.
　　　　　　　(2) The children were rough.
　　　　　　　(3) The children were spoiled.

　　　　　　　The children were delightful, but they were rough and spoiled.

a) (1) They looked at Clara.
　 (2) Clara was on the other side of the room.
　 (3) Clara was talking to the wives.

b) (1) A woman gets married.
　 (2) A woman has children.
　 (3) She doesn't pay any attention to her husband.

c) (1) When she woke up, she saw a large pastry.
　 (2) The pastry was decorated with whipped cream.
　 (3) The pastry was suspended in the air.

d) (1) I can see it happening.
　 (2) It is happening with my female students.
　 (3) It would be futile to warn them.

C. SUGGESTIONS FOR WRITING

1. Describe what happened to Clara by rewriting Joe's description of her in the past tense.
2. Describe someone you know who is not happy with his or her role in life.
3. Compare the daily activities of two women with different roles in your culture.

SEEING DOUBLE

Langston Hughes

*Langston Hughes (1902–1967) is best known for his
poetry and fiction, which deal with the life of the
black American.*

*The following selection was taken from a collection
of short stories called* The Best of Simple. *Simple,
who is the main character in these stories, is a talkative,
friendly fellow with a good sense of humor. Much of
the language of the selection is characteristic of general
informal conversation, but Hughes has also included
some vocabulary characteristic of the black community
of Simple and his friends. These terms have been
explained in the notes.*

"I wonder why it is we have two of one thing,
and only one of others."

"For instance?"

"We have two lungs," said Simple, "but only
one heart. Two eyes, but only one mouth. Two—"

"Feet, but only one body," I said.

"I was not going to say *feet,*" said Simple.
"But since you have taken the words out of my
mouth, go ahead."

"Human beings have two shoulders but only
one neck."

"And two ears but only one head," said Simple.

"What on earth would you want with two
heads?"

"I could sleep with one and stay awake with the other," explained Simple. "Just like I got two nostrils, I would also like to have two mouths, then I could eat with one mouth while I am talking with the other. Joyce always starts an argument while we are eating, anyhow. That Joyce can talk and eat all at once."

"Suppose Joyce had two mouths, too," I said. "She could double-talk you."

"I would not keep company with a woman that had two mouths," said Simple. "But I would like to have two myself."

"If you had two mouths, you would have to have two noses also," I said, "and it would not make such sense to have two noses, would it?"

"No," said Simple, "I reckon it wouldn't. Neither would I like to have two chins to have to shave. A chin is no use for a thing. But there is one thing I sure would like to have two of. Since I have—"

"Since you have two eyes, I know you would like to have two faces—one in front and one behind—so you could look at all those pretty women on the street both going and coming."

"That would be idealistic," said Simple, "but that is *not* what I was going to say. You always cut me off. So you go ahead and talk."

"I know you wish you had two stomachs," I said, "so you could eat more of Joyce's good cooking."

"No, I do *not* wish I had two stomachs," said Simple. "I can put away enough food in one belly to mighty near wreck my pocketbook—with prices as high as a cat's back in a dogfight. So I do not need two stomachs. Neither do I need two navels on the stomach I got. What use are they? But there is one thing I sure wish I had two of."

"Two gullets?" I asked.

"Two gullets is *not* what I wish I had at all," said Simple. "Let me talk! *I wish I had two brains.*"

"Two brains! Why?"

"So I could think with one, and let the other one rest, man, that's why. I am tired of trying to figure out how to get ahead in this world. If I had two brains, I could think with one brain while the other brain was asleep. I could plan with one while the other brain was drunk. I could think about the Dodgers with one, and my future with the other. As it is now, there is too much in this world for one brain to take care of alone. I have thought so much with my one brain that it is about wore out. In fact, I need a rest right now. So let's drink up and talk about something pleasant. Two beers are on me tonight. Draw up to the bar."

"I was just at the bar," I said, "and Tony has nothing but bottles tonight, no draft."

"Then, daddy-o, they're on *you*," said Simple. "I only got two dimes—and one of them is a Roosevelt dime I do not wish to spend. Had I been thinking, I would have remembered that Roosevelt dime. When I get my other brain, it will keep track of all such details."

GLOSS

taken the words out of my mouth: said the same thing that I was going to say

what on earth: intensified, dramatic way of saying *what*

just like I got: in the same way that I have

Joyce: a girl's name; Simple's girlfriend

all at once: at the same time

double-talk: here, the verb means to say twice as much and to confuse

keep company with: be a very close friend of—often with the intention of marriage

reckon: think

cut (someone) off: interrupt

mighty near: almost

wreck my pocketbook: cost all my money

man: a common contemporary expression in informal conversation
   used sometimes as a form of address
Dodgers: a famous American baseball team
wore out: very tired; the standard form would be *worn out*
(something is) on me: I'll pay
draw up: here, the phrase means *come*
nothing but: only
draft: draft beer—beer that is not bottled
daddy-o: an informal form of address to a man
Roosevelt dime: a dime with a face of Franklin D. Roosevelt on it.
   Roosevelt dimes were new in the late 1940s, when the story was
   written.
keep track of: remember

A. COMPREHENSION

1. What does Simple wonder about?
2. Why does Simple want two heads?
3. Why does Simple want two mouths?
4. What can Joyce do that Simple can't?
5. Does Simple want two noses?
6. What else doesn't Simple want?
7. Why doesn't Simple want two chins?
8. What does Simple's friend think of Joyce's cooking?
9. Why doesn't Simple want two stomachs?
10. What does Simple want most of all?
11. What could one brain do while the other was thinking?
12. What does Simple offer to buy his friend? What words does he use?
13. Why does Simple change his mind?

B. LANGUAGE EXERCISES

1. VOCABULARY

   a) Fill in the blanks using words from the list below. Some of
      the words may be used more than once.

asleep	idealistic	details
awake	pleasant	brains
drunk	arguments	future

If a man has two heads, one head can be _____

_____ while the other head can be _____. One

head can worry about the _____ of daily existence

while the other head can think about more _____

things. Of course, some heads don't have any _____

_____, and that makes it difficult to win _____.

b) Give another word or phrase similar in meaning that could replace the underlined words in the sentences below.
   (1) You have said the same thing that I was going to say.
   (2) Joyce always starts a fight while we are eating.
   (3) Joyce can talk and eat at the same time.
   (4) You always interrupt me.
   (5) He can eat enough food for ten people.
   (6) I am tired of trying to figure out how to succeed in this world.
   (7) Tony has only bottled beer.
   (8) My brain will remember all such details.

2. IF . . .

Tell what you would do if you had only one of various parts of your body.

Example: If I had only one *nostril,* I would need smaller handkerchiefs.

3. SAYINGS

a) Agree or disagree with the point of the following sayings:

(1) Two can live as cheaply as one.
(2) A bird in the hand is worth two in the bush.
(3) Blondes have twice as much fun.
b) Are there similar sayings in your culture?

4. I WONDER . . .

If Simple talked about other things, he might say, "I wonder why the sky is blue." Or, "I wonder why fire causes smoke."

a) Make up some "I wonder . . ." statements.
b) Ask your classmates for the answers to the "I wonder . . ." statements.

5. DESIGNS

Simple is interested in the design of the human body. If you had the opportunity to begin from the beginning, how would you design the human body? a car? a city? Draw your design and describe it.

Example: My ideal human body has one eye in front and one eye in back.

6. SENTENCE COMBINING

This is an exercise in combining three short sentences into one longer and better sentence. Your final sentence should have the same ideas as the original sentences, but you may make changes.

Example: (1) The children were delightful.
(2) The children were rough.
(3) The children were spoiled.

The children were delightful, but they were rough and spoiled.

a) (1) Simple doesn't want two chins.
(2) Simple doesn't want two noses.
(3) Simple doesn't want two navels.

b) (1) I would like two stomachs.
   (2) One stomach could eat.
   (3) The other stomach could rest.

c) (1) Some heads are large.
   (2) Some heads are beautiful.
   (3) Some heads don't have any brains.

d) (1) I would like to have two mouths.
   (2) I could eat with one mouth.
   (3) I could talk with the other mouth.

e) (1) I think about the high prices.
   (2) I think about my future.
   (3) These things make my brain tired.

f) (1) You would like two faces.
   (2) You would like one face in front and one face behind.
   (3) You would look at all the pretty women on the street.

g) (1) I have thought a lot with my one brain.
   (2) My brain is worn out.
   (3) I need a new brain.

h) (1) I wonder something.
   (2) We have two of some things.
   (3) We have only one of other things.

C. SUGGESTIONS FOR WRITING

1. This selection is a conversation. Summarize it and write it as a narrative.

2. Retell the story from the point of view of Tony, the bartender. You might want to begin like this:

   > When I came in to work tonight, Simple and his friend were sitting in a booth.

3. Describe ways in which friends treat (i.e., pay for) each other in your culture. For example, if a man and a woman were going around together, would the woman ever pay for the man?

4. Compare the customs of treating (i.e., paying for) others in your culture with those of another culture.

A CASE FOR THE UN

Miriam Allen de Ford

Miriam Allen de Ford (b. 1888) is an American writer whose stories, poems, and articles have appeared in magazines and anthologies. She has won many poetry prizes, and in 1961 and 1965 she won awards for her mystery stories.

The mystery story is a very popular form of fiction today. Each story usually has a murder, a detective who is the hero or heroine, and an unexpected ending. The selection below is taken from a story called "A Case for the UN," which was written in 1964. In this story a plane is flying over the Atlantic Ocean from New York to Ireland. After the passengers have gone to sleep, a man gets up and kills two people. Then he says that since the plane was not flying over any country, he cannot be accused of any crime.

At three o'clock in the morning they were over the mid-Atlantic.

It was then that the little man in the rear, Bartholomew Evans, got quietly to his feet. No one paid any attention to him; others had arisen from time to time and gone back to the lavatory.

Evans stepped forward silently until he stood in the aisle between Renée Blanc and Giuseppe Falconari, who were now sound asleep, their heads buried in pillows.

Very calmly and deliberately, Evans drew a

103

pistol from his pocket, and shot each of them through the head.

Immediately there was pandemonium. Startled passengers awoke, jumped up, cried out. Mavis ran to the cockpit, forgetting her shoes, and almost collided with Kemper as he opened the door and hurried to the scene.

The murderer made no attempt to move. He stood there with the smoking pistol still in his hand. Not a sound came from either of his victims; there was not even much blood. Both had been killed instantly.

The pilot took command at once.

"Please resume your seats," Kemper ordered, hoping his voice was steady. He had heard plenty of stories of sensational events on other planes, but this was his first and, he hoped, his last experience of this kind. "See to this lady," he added to Mavis; an elderly woman sitting nearby was in hysterics. Mavis, her legs trembling, ministered to the woman and got her quieted down. There was little noise otherwise; most of the passengers were too shocked to speak.

A heavy-set man stood up and started toward the murderer. Kemper stopped him with a gesture. The responsibility and the danger—were his.

"Give me the gun," he demanded of Evans.

The coolest person on board was the murderer.

"Certainly, Captain," Evans replied politely, placing the gun in Kemper's outstretched hand. "And you needn't tie me up. I'm not going to pull any doors open and jump out, or do anything foolish."

Unexpectedly somebody laughed. Someone else reached blindly for a paper bag and was sick in it.

"Ladies and gentlemen, please keep your seats," the pilot said, his voice steady now. "I know how distressing this must be for you, but there is nothing we can do until we arrive at Shannon.

Mavis, I think everybody could use a drink. But first get some blankets to cover these—these two people. And if you, madam, and you, sir, who were sitting next to them would find places elsewhere—"

The suggestion was unnecessary; the victims' neighbors were already hunched in seats farther away.

"Now"—Kemper turned to the still unmoving Evans—"I shall have you placed under guard until I can turn you over to the Eire authorities when we land. Our copilot will have wired ahead, and the police will have been notified. They'll be waiting for you. Now, if two of you gentlemen will volunteer to keep an eye on him—"

The burly man and another stepped forward.

Bartholomew Evans smiled.

"You know, Captain," he said conversationally, "I happen to be a lawyer, and I know a few things that you don't. For instance, though an aircraft in flight has the legal status of a ship at sea, its pilot does not have the power of arrest and detention that a ship's captain has. You have no right whatever to hold or guard me.

"And the authorities you say will be waiting to apprehend me can do nothing whatever. Eire has no jurisdiction over me. I waited deliberately to do my—deed until we were over the mid-Atlantic. My whole action depended on the fact that no nation in the world has jurisdiction in this matter. I've made very sure of the law. There is *nowhere* I can be held, *nowhere* I can be tried. There is no such thing as a code of international criminal air law, nor is there any Air Police Force."

GLOSS

sound asleep: sleeping deeply
Mavis: the stewardess
Kemper: the pilot of the plane
see to (someone): help

at once: immediately
keep your seats: remain in your seats
Shannon: the international airport in Ireland
turn you over: give you
Eire: Irish (Gaelic word)
keep an eye on: watch
be tried: have a trial

A. COMPREHENSION

1. At what time did the murder happen?
2. Where was the plane at the time of the murder?
3. Who was watching Evans?
4. Where had Evans been sitting?
5. How did Evans kill the couple?
6. What was the couple doing when Evans killed them?
7. How did the passengers react when they heard the shots?
8. What did the stewardess do?
9. What did Evans do?
10. Who took command? What did he do?
11. Who did Mavis help? Why?
12. Why wasn't there much noise on the plane?
13. How did the pilot get the gun from the murderer?
14. Did the Captain tie Evans up?
15. What did the pilot tell the passengers to do?
16. What did the pilot tell Mavis to do?
17. What did the pilot intend to do with the murderer?
18. Was Evans worried about being arrested? Why?
19. Why did the murderer wait until the plane was over the Atlantic before he killed his victims?

B. LANGUAGE EXERCISES

1. VOCABULARY

Fill in the blanks using words from the lists on the next page. Some of the words may be used more than once.

hysterics	pay attention to	outstretched
laughter	resume	shocked
cover	see to	cool
collided with	tied up	blindly
jumped up	hunched	sound

When the shots sounded, most of the passengers

were _____ asleep. The stewardess _____

from her seat and ran to the cockpit. The pilot told her

to _____ an old woman who was in _____.

The pilot then told the passengers to _____ their

seats. Most of the passengers were too _____ to

speak.

awoke	foolish	instantly
depend on	shocked	quietly
started	calmly	silently
volunteer	deliberately	

A man said to Evans, "I _____ when you

_____ to walk _____ down the aisle of

the plane. You took your gun out _____ and shot

those people _____. You are _____ if you

think you can _____ a legal technicality to escape.

I am _____ at your act and I will _____

my help to the police."

2. CONNECTING IDEAS

The following sentences are not in a normal order. Arrange them in an order that shows how the ideas are connected. You may connect sentences if you want to.

a)   (1) At that moment he stood up.
        (2) She started to walk toward him.
        (3) He looked innocent.
        (4) When she returned to the cabin she looked at the man in the rear seat.
        (5) But she thought that she should talk to him anyhow.
        (6) He was a middle-aged man with glasses.
        (7) He was reading a newspaper.
b)   (1) The pilot took command at once.
        (2) There was pandemonium.
        (3) The man shot two passengers.
        (4) The murderer made no attempt to move.
        (5) Most of the passengers were sound asleep.
        (6) A man got up from the rear of the plane.
        (7) The murderer said that no country had jurisdiction over him.
        (8) A burly man volunteered to guard the murderer.
        (9) The pilot demanded the gun from the murderer.
     (10) The stewardess quieted down a hysterical woman.

3. REACTIONS TO FEAR

a) People react to fear in different ways. What are the ways the people in the story reacted?

Example: Two people hunched in their seats.

b) What are some other things that people do when they are afraid?

4. VARYING THE THEME

a) What could the murderer have done after he shot the couple?

b) What could have happened if the pilot had not taken command at once?

c) What could have happened if the victims had awakened before they were shot?

d) What might have happened if the murderer had not been the coolest person on board?

5. TOO_____TO DO IT

"Most of the passengers were too *shocked* to speak." What other adjectives could you use to describe the passengers?

6. PUZZLES AND MYSTERIES

a) Many detective stories make the readers think of different solutions. A famous children's puzzle does too. Try this.

There was a man who had to take a wolf, a goat, and a cabbage across a river. His boat was very small; it would hold only the man and *one other thing*. What could the man do? How could he take the wolf, the goat, and the cabbage across the river, one at a time, so that the wolf wouldn't eat the goat and the goat wouldn't eat the cabbage?

A hint: First, the man took the goat across.

(For the answer, see page 129.)

b) If you solved that puzzle, try this one.

John weighed 198 pounds. He was walking along the road carrying three coconuts. Each coconut weighed one pound. He came to a bridge, and he saw a sign there. The sign read: This bridge can support only 200 pounds. How did John get across the bridge in one trip with his three coconuts?

(For the answer, see page 129.)

7. SENTENCE COMBINING

This is an exercise in combining three short sentences into one longer and better sentence. Your final sentence should have the same ideas as the original sentences, but you may make changes.

Example: (1) The children were delightful.
(2) The children were rough.
(3) The children were spoiled.

The children were delightful, but they were rough and spoiled.

a) (1) The stewardess stood in the aisle.
(2) The stewardess was between two passengers.
(3) The two passengers were asleep.
b) (1) No one paid any attention to the man.
(2) No one paid any attention to the woman.
(3) The man and the woman were hunched up in their seats.
c) (1) The murderer took a pistol from his pocket.
(2) The murderer was calm and deliberate.
(3) The murderer shot them both.
d) (1) The stewardess's legs were trembling.
(2) The stewardess helped the woman.
(3) The stewardess quieted the woman down.
e) (1) I'm not going to open any doors.
(2) I'm not going to jump out.
(3) I'm not going to do anything foolish.

C. SUGGESTIONS FOR WRITING

1. Describe the most frightening experience you have had on an airplane or on any other means of transportation.
2. Most airports now have security measures to stop hijacking. How effective are these measures? What other things could be done?
3. What do you think happened at the end of the story? Write your own conclusion. (See page 129 to find out what actually happened.)

VOCABULARY REVIEW

Directions: Draw a circle around the answer that is most similar in meaning to the word or words in *italics*.

Example: There was a *crowd* in the market-place.
a) a small number of people
b) a place to buy food
c) a large number of people
d) a place to eat food

A large number of people is the correct answer. There is a circle around the words *a large number of people*.

1. The children were rough and *spoiled*.
   a) curious
   b) dirty
   c) not well-behaved
   d) not very happy

2. His *parents* were strict.
   a) father's family
   b) cousins
   c) mother's family
   d) mother and father

3. The nurse looked at Mama *curiously*.
   a) strangely
   b) disapprovingly
   c) finally
   d) politely

4. The nurse stared at Mama with *amazement.*
   a) pride
   b) surprise
   c) delight
   d) brightness

5. I heard sounds more *distinctly* at that time.
   a) mysteriously
   b) clearly
   c) nervously
   d) quietly

6. We would have *vanished* from the earth long ago.
   a) nourished
   b) appeared
   c) gone
   d) discovered

7. In every house there *ought to* be an art table.
   a) will
   b) could
   c) has to
   d) should

8. Nobody really looks at *familiar* things.
   a) natural
   b) belonging to the family
   c) common
   d) arranged

9. It's *chilly* when you get up in the morning.
   a) cool
   b) early
   c) clear
   d) fertile

10. In the old days, his father was *sober.*
    a) formal
    b) not drunk
    c) polite
    d) not rich

11. It was *rare* that their mother would let them take off their shirts.
    a) expected
    b) unusual
    c) arranged
    d) often

12. He found things everyone had *overlooked.*
    a) not seen
    b) looked for
    c) seen from above
    d) considered

13. He wanted to stay at a *deserted* beach.
    a) sandy
    b) covered
    c) decorated
    d) empty

14. Their voices were *gentle.*
    a) heavy
    b) empty
    c) alive
    d) kind

15. I had *plenty* of time to make the train.
    a) not enough
    b) a lot of
    c) a little
    d) exactly enough

16. Everyone *wondered* about his speech.
    a) was proud
    b) was excited
    c) was delighted
    d) was curious

17. The girl with the flossy fringe *giggled.*
    a) laughed
    b) was sick
    c) cried
    d) was unhappy

18. You never see the same *customer* twice.
    a) person who repairs things
    b) person who sells things
    c) person who makes things
    d) person who buys things

19. Mr. Olliphant showed me some of the *finer* points of drawing.
    a) more basic
    b) more complex
    c) more formal
    d) stranger

20. I was *jostled* by a woman in the crowd.
    a) threatened
    b) surprised
    c) pushed
    d) discovered

21. I will *avoid* my fate.
    a) escape
    b) change
    c) take over
    d) wait for

22. It was only a *start* of surprise.
    a) beginning
    b) slow movement
    c) thought
    d) sudden movement

23. I was *astonished* to see him in Bagdad.
    a) delighted
    b) proud
    c) surprised
    d) afraid

24. Even an *ordinary* person like myself changes a lot.
    a) different
    b) impatient
    c) calm
    d) normal

25. Most of the passengers were too *shocked* to speak.
    a) tired
    b) surprised
    c) cold
    d) afraid

26. The *burly* man stepped forward.
    a) smiling
    b) little
    c) heavy-set
    d) startled

27. He walked forward *deliberately*.
    a) instantly
    b) silently
    c) slowly
    d) nervously

28. She's *hollow* inside.
    a) full
    b) empty
    c) sick
    d) healthy

29. It would be *futile* to warn them.
    a) useless
    b) foolish
    c) useful
    d) necessary

30. The little man was in the *rear* of the plane.
    a) back
    b) middle
    c) front
    d) lavatory

31. As he shot them, he was *calm*.
    a) excited
    b) angry
    c) shocked
    d) quiet

32. Marian had a *fleeting* vision of a pastry.
    a) idealistic
    b) delightful
    c) feminine
    d) quick

33. The old man *muttered* to himself.
    a) confessed
    b) spoke in a low voice
    c) frowned
    d) spoke in a high voice

34. My heart *thumped* a little.
    a) beat heavily
    b) beat more easily
    c) beat quietly
    d) beat more slowly

35. The rolling hills *beckoned him.*
    a) called to
    b) interested
    c) threatened
    d) answered

36. The land is *nourished* by the spring rains.
    a) chilled
    b) cleaned
    c) invaded
    d) fed

37. I *intended* to stay there only for a short time, but I stayed longer.
    a) arranged
    b) used
    c) figured out
    d) planned

38. He liked to collect *trash.*
    a) things which were worth a lot.
    b) things which were very old.
    c) things which were new.
    d) things which were not worth much.

39. She cleaned the floors with a *damp* mop.
   a) dirty
   b) clean
   c) dry
   d) wet

40. She pushed the mop *vigorously*.
   a) with pleasure
   b) with freedom
   c) with difficulty
   d) with strength

41. Stephen was *a loner* at college.
   a) without enemies
   b) living in one room
   c) not married
   d) without friends

42. She always starts *an argument* while we are eating.
   a) a conversation
   b) a fight
   c) a story
   d) a prayer

43. Everything at home was *neat*.
   a) odd
   b) arranged
   c) old
   d) predictable

44. My mother *fulfilled* her many duties.
   a) enjoyed
   b) completed
   c) preserved
   d) discovered

45. Sometimes I was full of *misery*.
   a) joy
   b) impatience
   c) loneliness
   d) unhappiness

46. He *inhaled* the cigarette smoke.
   a) breathed in
   b) coughed
   c) breathed out
   d) blew

47. He is a *vain* boy.
   a) having a very high opinion of himself.
   b) having a feeling of pain
   c) having a very low opinion of himself
   d) having a feeling of relief

48. She *frowned* when she saw the picture.
   a) looked happy
   b) made a noise through her nose
   c) looked unhappy
   d) giggled

49. Her words sounded *clipped*.
   a) clear
   b) shortened
   c) not distinct
   d) lengthened

50. It was a *formal* meeting.
   a) familiar
   b) not planned
   c) strict
   d) according to rules

IDIOM REVIEW

Directions: Draw a circle around the answer that is most similar in meaning to the word or words in *italics*.

Example: I *called up* an old friend yesterday.
a) telephoned
b) visited
c) met
d) saw

Telephoned is the correct answer. There is a circle around the word *telephoned*.

1. *Up to* this evening, everything had been delightful.
   a) Throughout
   b) After
   c) Until
   d) Except

2. When I was *about* twelve, I ran away from home.
   a) more than
   b) approximately
   c) less than
   d) exactly

3. I watched until *she was out of sight*.
   a) she could not see
   b) she was outside
   c) I could not see her
   d) I saw her

119

4. She was going to *break in* a new girl.
   a) hurt
   b) look for
   c) train
   d) pay

5. *At last* we went out and stood on the lawn.
   a) Finally
   b) In the afternoon
   c) First
   d) In the evening

6. There is always so much *going on*.
   a) happening
   b) disappearing
   c) traveling
   d) feeling

7. His *old man* would sleep away the afternoon.
   a) father
   b) servant
   c) grandfather
   d) master

8. *By some chance* we are all here at the same time.
   a) Fortunately
   b) Because of a plan
   c) Accidentally
   d) Because of a change

9. He *tore up* the steps toward the gate.
   a) started
   b) turned
   c) walked
   d) ran

10. As he spoke to the guard, he became *hot under the collar*.
    a) excited
    b) disapproving
    c) spoiled
    d) rough

11. *No wonder* the Italians are happy.
    a) It is surprising
    b) It is wonderful
    c) It is not surprising
    d) It is not wonderful

12. Miss Adams had *smelled a rat.*
    a) become suspicious
    b) confessed
    c) made a mistake
    d) disapproved

13. He *went in for* Eastern religions.
    a) became interested in
    b) visited
    c) lost interest in
    d) depended on

14. I *longed for* something as beautiful as the mountains.
    a) waited for
    b) avoided
    c) wanted
    d) thought of

15. In New York you're really *dealing with* the public.
    a) meeting
    b) watching
    c) waiting for
    d) enjoying

16. School *is over* for the year.
    a) will last
    b) is finished
    c) is free
    d) has begun

17. Joseph would *call on* me sometimes.
    a) telephone
    b) visit
    c) intrude on
    d) give attention to

18. He has never *gotten through* the novel *Ulysses*.
    a) understood
    b) outgrown
    c) discussed
    d) finished

19. You have *taken the words out of my mouth*.
    a) said something that I don't agree with
    b) said the same thing that I was going to say
    c) not given me permission to speak
    d) not asked permission to speak

20. Joyce can talk and eat *all at once*.
    a) one time
    b) not at the same time
    c) more than one time
    d) at the same time

21. *The beers are on me.*
    a) I am covered with beer.
    b) The beers are for me.
    c) I will pay for the beers.
    d) You should pay for the beers.

22. It is difficult to *keep track of* the details.
    a) summarize
    b) forget
    c) change
    d) remember

23. The passengers were *sound asleep*.
    a) sleeping deeply
    b) making noise while they were sleeping
    c) sleeping very lightly
    d) sleeping quietly

24. It will *do you good* to change jobs.
    a) be hard for you
    b) make you rich
    c) be easy for you
    d) be good for you

25. The stewardess *kept an eye on* the passenger.
    a) watched
    b) saw
    c) accused
    d) aroused

26. The criminal was *turned over to* the police.
    a) covered by
    b) given to
    c) taken from
    d) jostled by

27. The pilot took command *at once*.
    a) immediately
    b) alone
    c) after a while
    d) at one o'clock

28. The actor *ran over* the scene many times.
    a) hurried
    b) left
    c) discussed
    d) rehearsed

29. I never *figured out* what was on the paper.
    a) understood
    b) saw
    c) covered
    d) drew

30. Was he *sick of* work?
    a) hurt by
    b) looking for
    c) absent from
    d) unhappy with

31. Everything was *set up* early.
    a) wakened
    b) decorated
    c) arranged
    d) cleaned

32. The teacher told the students to *keep their seats*.
    a) go to their seats
    b) leave their seats alone
    c) remain in their seats
    d) put their seats in a line

COMPREHENSION REVIEW

Directions: Draw a circle around the answer that best completes
the statement or answers the question.

1. In "The Oyster," how did Gopal feel about his experience in
   Europe?
   a) The experience did not affect him at all.
   b) The experience made him very happy.
   c) The experience made him both happy and sad.
   d) The experience made him very sad.

2. In "How My Love Was Sawed in Half," the author did something that his family did not expect him to do. What was it?
   a) He drank a lot of wine.
   b) He arranged his room neatly.
   c) He decided not to go to camp.
   d) He worked in a carnival.

3. In "Mama and the Hospital," Mama figured out
   a) how to visit Dagmar.
   b) how to clean the floors.
   c) what was wrong with Dagmar.
   d) how to get Dagmar out of the hospital.

4. The author of "In a Strange Town" particularly enjoyed experiences that
   a) included pleasant sounds.
   b) made him curious.
   c) happened in foreign places.
   d) took place many years ago.

5. In "The Good Old Days," the advice of the Italian chief to the Americans was to
   a) answer letters right away.
   b) get more secretaries.
   c) use more equipment.
   d) work a little slower.

6. In which of the following stories is there a problem between a father and son?
   a) "Knoxville: Summer 1915"
   b) "Like the Lion's Tooth"
   c) "Leaf"
   d) "The Oyster"

7. Which of the following phrases best describes Simple, the main character in "Seeing Double"?
   a) He has bad eyes.
   b) He has a good sense of humor.
   c) He is always drunk.
   d) He likes to start arguments.

8. In "Not Goin' Anywhere," Estelle Wowak dreams of leaving home because she wants to
   a) become an actress.
   b) live in a small town.
   c) join a carnival.
   d) live in a big city.

9. The narrator in Anderson's "In a Strange Town" could best be described as
   a) threatening.
   b) curious.
   c) free.
   d) sad.

10. What did the teacher in "The Vivisector" make Hurtle do?
   a) write a composition.
   b) talk to the rector.
   c) draw an elephant.
   d) throw his paper in the basket.

11. In "The Edible Woman," Joe thought that after marriage women
    a) became happier.
    b) became more independent.
    c) lost their personalities.
    d) had more opportunities for college.

12. In "Death Speaks," Death appears to the characters in the form of a
    a) woman.
    b) servant.
    c) merchant.
    d) horse.

13. In "A Case for the UN," Evans committed a murder over the Atlantic because
    a) he was able to take a gun from the pilot.
    b) he thought he couldn't be tried for the crime.
    c) he was attacked by a burly man.
    d) he discovered his enemies were on the plane.

14. The author of "Jones Beach" thought that people
    a) realized that they were free.
    b) were not born free.
    c) were not really free.
    d) did not realize that they were free.

15. Why did the father in "Leaf" want to have an art table in his house?
    a) His son liked art very much.
    b) He wanted to put fashionable drawings on it.
    c) He wanted to put familiar objects on it.
    d) His son used to find interesting objects on the beach.

16. The life that the narrator in "The Man with the Dog" is living now could best be described as
    a) miserable.
    b) peaceful.
    c) impatient.
    d) fashionable.

17. In "Like the Lion's Tooth," what did Ben like to do when his family went to the beach?
    a) He liked to swim far out.
    b) He liked to find things in the sand.
    c) He liked to sleep away the afternoon.
    d) He liked to cover himself with sand.

18. In "The Return," Joseph and Steven both enjoyed
    a) reading books aloud.
    b) discussing *Ulysses.*
    c) going to church.
    d) eating a lot.

19. In "Knoxville: Summer 1915," the feelings of the boy toward his family could be described as
    a) hate.
    b) love.
    c) curiosity.
    d) amazement.

20. Who of the following did not attend a university or college?
    a) Clara
    b) Steven
    c) Gopal
    d) Hurtle

SOLUTIONS

1. What is the relationship between the boy and the doctor?

   The doctor is the mother of the boy.

2. How did the man get the wolf, the goat, and the cabbage across the river?

   a. He took the goat over.
   b. He took the wolf over and he took the goat back.
   c. He took the cabbage over (leaving the goat behind).
   d. He went back and got the goat.

   ### Or

   a. He took the goat over.
   b. He took the cabbage over and he took the goat back.
   c. He took the wolf over (leaving the goat behind).
   d. He went back and got the goat.

3. How did John get across the bridge with his three coconuts?

   He juggled them as he went across.

4. How does the story "A Case for the UN" end?

   Evans was right. The police couldn't arrest him for murder. But Evans had forgotten that he had planned the murder in New York with the help of a friend. Planning a murder, which is a form of conspiracy, is also a serious crime. Therefore, when the plane landed, the police arrested Evans and sent him back to New York where he had committed the crime of conspiracy.